Wow! This is Sugarfree

Artwork by Mary Yoder

First Printing March 1999
Second Printing September 1999
Third Printing January 2000
Fourth Printing July 2000
Fifth Printing June 2001
Sixth Printing March 2002
Seventh Printing July 2002
Eighth Printing December 2002
Ninth Printing May 2003
Tenth Printing September 2003
Eleventh Printing January 2004 (Revised)
Twelfth Printing June 2004
Thirteenth Printing May 2005
Fourteenth Printing June 2006
Fifteenth Printing May 2007
Sixteenth Printing January 2008
Seventeenth Printing October 2008

ISBN 0-9711105-0-6

For more copies contact:
Apple View Publications
4495 Cutter Road
Apple Creek, OH 44606-9641

2673 Township Road 421
Sugarcreek, OH 44681

Carlisle Printing
OF WALNUT CREEK Ind.

Expressions of Appreciation

We thank all our friends for the prompting and encouragement they have given us in beginning this book.

A special thanks to our husbands for their confidence and support in our taking on this project; also for their patience and understanding during this busy time.

We are grateful to our families for patiently "taste testing" the many foods while the recipes were being perfected. Diane, Darla, and Dorisa were invaluable in assisting, by carefully measuring and experimenting with these many recipes.

We extend our sincere appreciation to our friend, Elaine Troyer, for her time and patience in getting us started, and also for her suggestions and assistance along the way. Without her help, the book likely would not have materialized.

Introduction

Over the years I have had many requests for my recipes. Many times I was asked, "Why don't you write a cookbook?" An epidemic seems to be sweeping our nation. Many are discovering they have a sugar intolerance, or are allergic to certain foods. The symptoms may be varied: tired, headaches, blurred vision, depression, etc.

Also, people are becoming more aware of the dangers of eating so much refined, processed food containing additives and preservatives. They want real food the way God made it. But it is hard to change. Our taste buds have been trained to like soft, sweet, gooey foods.

To keep the family from becoming defensive, a slow approach may need to be taken, such as, only one "different" food served per meal. It may take a few tries before it is appreciated. *Check the section in back of the book on **"Making the Transition"** from unhealthy to healthy eating.*

Rather than trying to hide nutritious ingredients in foods, instill in your family the reason for eating whole nutritious foods, both the health benefits they will reap when adults, and also the economic side of it - grocery bills and doctor bills are lower.

While writing this book, I discovered I am unable to follow a recipe. I always need to improve it somehow! This makes cooking enjoyable. Don't be afraid to experiment. We all have different tastes and styles.

In my childhood home my mother and brother were on sugar free diets. My father and brother were both allergic to wheat, so I was used to this type of diet. After I married, I began to cook like "everybody else does". I gained 20 pounds in a short time.

Some years later we became aware of the fact that my husband could no longer tolerate sugar. He was suffering from frequent headaches and depression. When we discontinued using sugar, I automatically lost the 20 pounds again, and his depression and headaches went away (unless he cheated).

It took our family a number of years to get to the place where we don't use sweeteners. Experimenting and getting used to less and less sweetener took approximately 10 years! Today we use applesauce, pureed fruits, fruit juices, and dried fruits.

At first we cut back from the amount of sugar asked for in recipes. Next we used Sweet-N-Lo for a while. Then a nurse warned us of the danger of giving children artificial sweeteners, so we experimented with a variety of natural sweeteners.

You will find recipes in this book that call for a sweetener, then says "optional". We do not use it, although we did during the transitional years.

Our first two children were highly allergic to milk when babies - even goat milk. They still are somewhat sensitive to it. Since we eliminate milk and white flour from their daily diets, they don't have chronic colds and flu symptoms in the wintertime anymore. However we still use butter and cheese in foods. In the summer they drink milk with no ill effects.

At one time we were going to the doctor quite often. We were putting ear drops in ears nearly every night and getting nowhere. Now our doctor only needs to see us for emergency type situations.

While working on this cookbook we discovered one of our children was allergic to soy. After eating an unknown amount of TVP (texturized vegetable protein), she broke out in hives - small red dots on her face and hands mostly. For several weeks after that, she would again break out occasionally in a small patch of hives, always at mealtime. Upon investigation we discovered the culprit always to be soy products such as soy, soya, and lecithin hiding in various food items I used in cooking.

During these weeks she was also aggressive, irritable, and quarrelsome. She had a glint in her eyes; a driving force, causing her to look for something destructive or mean to do to someone or something, and then laughing about it. We had observed this behavior in the past many times, but never associated it with food allergy.

When the soy was taken out of her diet, she was again the sweetest little girl - looking for ways to please us, and so pleasant to be around. A miracle had happened!

Are you on a restricted diet? Or are you concerned about your family's health? Or perhaps just curious? I hope this book will prove to be helpful to you.

Deborah Steiner

Eleventh Printing, PS. Our previous printings used fruit source and barley malt for a sweetener. However, the fruit source company discontinued packaging fruit source for retail sale. We have replaced fruit source with stevia. Stevia does not affect blood sugar levels. Stevia is a plant and can be found in green (stevia herb) or white (stevia extract) powder form. We use green stevia. Use about half as much if using white stevia. Beware, stevia extract or Stevia Blend is bleached and sometimes has other ingredients added such as Maltodextrin. Be sure to check the label.

Because of the bad publicity canola oil has been receiving, we have replaced canola oil with olive oil.

Our sincere thanks to all of you who have so graciously written or called to express appreciation for the cookbook, and how it has helped you. You are a real encouragement to us!

Deborah and Mary

--Charts--

WEIGHTS AND MEASURES

3 teaspoons = 1 tablespoon

12 teaspoons = $\frac{1}{4}$ cup

4 tablespoons = $\frac{1}{4}$ cup

$5\frac{1}{3}$ tablespoons = $\frac{1}{3}$ cup

8 tablespoons = $\frac{1}{2}$ cup

$10\frac{2}{3}$ tablespoons = $\frac{2}{3}$ cup

12 tablespoons = $\frac{3}{4}$ cup

14 tablespoons = $\frac{7}{8}$ cup

16 tablespoons = 1 cup

2 tablespoons = 1 liquid ounce

1 cup = $\frac{1}{2}$ pint

2 cups = 1 pint

4 cups = 1 quart

4 quarts = 1 gallon

8 quarts = 1 peck

4 pecks = 1 bushel

16 ounces = 1 pound

COOKED FOOD MEASUREMENTS

1 cup uncooked rice = 3 cups cooked

$\frac{1}{3}$ cup uncooked lentils = 1 cup cooked

SUBSTITUTIONS

1 Tbsp. cornstarch = 2 Tbsp. flour or 1½ Tbsp. quick cooking tapioca

1 cup sour milk
   (or)
1 cup buttermilk = 1 Tbsp. lemon juice or vinegar + enough sweet milk
to equal 1 cup

1 tsp. baking powder = ¼ tsp. baking soda + ½ tsp. cream of tartar

3 Tbsp. carob powder + 2 Tbsp. butter or fruit juice conc. = 1 oz. unsweetened baking chocolate

STEVIA CONVERSION CHART

Sugar	Stevia Herb (green)	Liquid Stevia
1 cup	1 tsp.	1 tsp.
1 Tbsp.	⅛ tsp.	6 drops
1 tsp.	pinch	2 drops

Barley Malt	Stevia Herb (green)	Liquid Stevia
¼ cup	1 tsp.	1 tsp.

Note: Stevia Extract (white) varies in sweetness.
Try one-half or less of the amount you would use of the Stevia Herb (green).

ABBREVIATIONS

Tbsp. = tablespoon
tsp. = teaspoon
oz. = ounce
lb. = pound
qt. = quart
pt. = pint
opt. = optional

Table of Contents

(continued)

Breakfasts
and
Beverages

APPLE COFFEE CAKE

Mix, then set aside:

1 qt. apple pie filling

2 tsp. cinnamon

Beat:

3 eggs
1 Tbsp. barley malt or ¼ tsp.
                  stevia
½ cup butter or olive oil
1½ cups milk or apple juice

3 cups whole grain flour
2 tsp. baking soda
1 tsp. cream of tartar
1 tsp. salt

Pour ½ of batter into greased 9 x 13" pan. Spoon ½ of the pie filling over batter. Repeat with remaining batter and pie filling. Sprinkle chopped walnuts and date sugar over top. Drizzle with melted butter. Bake at 350° F. for 45 - 55 min.

Spiritual nugget:
Let **prayer** be the key to the day and the bolt to the night.

OVERNIGHT COFFEE CAKE

Beat:
2 eggs
Add:
¼ cup barley malt or 1 tsp.
               stevia, opt.
2 cups whole grain flour
½ tsp. salt

⅔ cup butter or olive oil

1 tsp. cinnamon
1 tsp. baking soda
1 tsp. baking powder
1 cup apple juice

Mix and pour into greased 8 x 12" pan.

Topping - mix all together:
1 Tbsp. date sugar, opt.
½ tsp. cinnamon
¼ tsp. nutmeg

¼ cup chopped nuts
¾ cup chopped dates

Sprinkle on top of batter. Cover and refrigerate 8 hrs. or overnight. Uncover, and bake at 350° F. for 35 - 40 min.

BLUEBERRY COFFEE CAKE

2 eggs
3 cups whole grain flour
1 tsp. salt
2 tsp. baking soda
1 cup apple juice

²/₃ cup olive oil
¹/₄ cup barley malt or
    1 tsp. stevia, opt.
¹/₂ tsp. cream of tartar
2 tsp. baking powder

Mix all ingredients, then fold in:
2 cups blueberries   1 cup nuts
    Pour in 9 x 13" pan.

Mix together and sprinkle over top:
3 Tbsp. butter
¹/₄ cup date sugar, opt.
¹/₃ cup chopped nuts

³/₄ tsp. cinnamon
¹/₃ cup whole grain flour

Bake at 350° F. for 40 - 45 minutes. Allow to cool before serving or it will be crumbly.

FRENCH TOAST, DAIRY FREE

7 slices thin whole grain bread
5 eggs, slightly beaten
1 tsp. cinnamon
1 tsp. vanilla extract

Combine all ingredients except bread. Dip bread in mixture, allow to soak a little. Then place in greased preheated pan. Brown on both sides. Do not cover.

Serve with Pancake Syrup *(page 9)*, or instead of bread use Date Nut Bread *(see recipe)* and eat plain.

GRAPENUTS

1 egg
1 cup rolled oats
2 tsp. baking soda
1/2 cup applesauce
1 tsp. maple flavoring

3 cups whole grain flour
1/2 tsp. salt
1 tsp. cream of tartar
2 cups apple juice

Mix all ingredients. Bake in 8 x 12" greased pan at 350° F. for 35 min. Allow to cool. Crumble and put on cookie sheets in thin layer. Stir occasionally and mash with fork during baking to make crumbs finer. Bake in 250° F. oven until dry and crunchy. Crack oven door open with spoon handle in top edge of oven door to allow steam to escape. May be stored at room temperature up to a week.

> **Hint:**
> Granola may be stored at room temperature.
> When making large batches, store extra containers in the refrigerator.

GRANOLA

6 cups oatmeal
1 1/2 cups oat bran
1 cup chopped nuts or
        sunflower seeds
1 1/2 tsp. vanilla
1/4 tsp. cinnamon

3/4 cup wheat germ
1/2 cup coconut
1 cup applesauce
1/4 cup olive oil
1/4 cup barley malt or
        1 tsp. stevia (opt.)

Mix dry ingredients. Then mix rest of ingredients and stir into dry ingredients. Bake at 350° F. for 40 minutes, stirring every 10 - 15 min. Add 1 1/2 cups raisins when done.

> Slivered or sliced almonds are delicious in granola.

PEANUT BUTTER GRANOLA

6 cups oatmeal
1/2 cup wheat germ
1/2 cup applesauce
2 Tbsp. olive oil
2/3 cup peanut butter

2 cups oat bran
1/2 cup chopped nuts or
        sunflower seeds
1 tsp. vanilla
1 cup raisins

Mix first four ingredients. In a measuring cup, combine wet ingredients. Stir into dry ingredients. Bake at 325° F. for 45 min. Stir every 10 minutes. Add raisins after cooled.

> **Hint: Allergic to milk?**
> Use fruit juice in cereal instead of milk. Fruit is delicious with cereal.

AUTUMN OATMEAL

1½ cups water
1 cup rolled oats
¼ tsp. cinnamon
pinch of salt

1 cup apple juice or water
¼ cup oat bran
1 cup fresh sweet apples, diced

In a saucepan, combine the liquids. Bring to a boil. Reduce heat to low. Stir in the rest of the ingredients. Simmer until desired consistency (approx. 5 - 10 min.).

Serve with milk or fruit if desired.

Note: Raisins may be substituted for apples.

BAKED OATMEAL

Mix:

¼ cup olive oil
2 eggs

1 cup apple juice

Add:

2 cups oatmeal
2 tsp. baking powder
½ tsp. vanilla
½ cup raisins (opt.)

1 cup oat bran
pinch of salt
¼ tsp. cinnamon

Pour into 9 x 13" greased pan.
Bake at 350° F. for 30 - 40 min. or until brown.   8 servings

EASY OMELET

Saute in heated, well buttered skillet any or all of the following:

shredded or sliced potatoes
   (If not cooked, allow to
   soften before adding
   rest of ingredients)
green peppers

wieners
bread crumbs
mushrooms
onions
salt

Break desired amount of eggs into pan. Stir and cover. Cook over medium heat, stirring frequently, until just set. Lay Velveeta cheese slices or shredded cheddar cheese over ½ of the eggs. Fold other half over top.

FIX AHEAD SCRAMBLED EGGS

4 wieners, diced
2 Tbsp. butter
1 - 3 oz. can mushrooms, drained

1 small onion
12 eggs, beaten

In a large skillet, saute wieners and onion in butter. Add eggs. Scramble until just set. Remove from heat and spread mushrooms over top.

CHEESE SAUCE:

2 Tbsp. butter
$1/2$ tsp. salt
2 cups milk

2 Tbsp. whole grain flour
$1/8$ tsp. pepper
1 cup grated cheddar cheese

Melt butter, blend in flour, salt and pepper. Add milk gradually. Cook and stir constantly until bubbly. Stir in cheese until melted. Fold cheese sauce into cooked eggs. Place in 8 x 12" baking dish. Combine topping ingredients and sprinkle over eggs.

TOPPING:

4 Tbsp. butter, melted
$1/8$ tsp. paprika

$2^1/2$ cups whole grain bread crumbs

Cover and refrigerate overnight until 30 minutes before baking. Bake uncovered at 350° F. for 30 minutes.   4 - 6 servings

Hint:
   Diced, unpeeled zucchini is good in scrambled eggs. Brown the zucchini in buttered fry pan. Add eggs. When set sprinkle with cheese.

BLUEBERRY BRAN PANCAKES

Combine:
$1/2$ cup bran
$3/4$ cup whole grain flour
$1/2$ cup fresh or thawed blueberries

1 tsp. baking powder
$1/2$ tsp. baking soda

Combine in another bowl:
1 beaten egg
$3/4$ cup buttermilk or
         apple juice

2 Tbsp. frozen orange juice
                concentrate

Add wet ingredients to dry and use large spatula to combine. (Don't overmix. About 10 strokes is sufficient.)   Makes 8 - 10 pancakes.

Leftover pancakes?
   Leftover pancakes are good warmed up in toaster or spread flat on cookie sheet and toasted in oven.

WHOLE GRAIN PANCAKES

2 eggs, beaten
3 tsp. baking soda
2 cups apple juice

2 cups whole grain flour
1 tsp. salt
6 Tbsp. olive oil

Combine all ingredients until just mixed. Pour onto hot greased pan, turning once.   Makes 10 - 12 pancakes

Hint:
    Our children love waffles with peanut butter.

OATMEAL WAFFLES

6 Tbsp. butter, melted
1$\frac{1}{2}$ cups whole grain flour
$\frac{1}{2}$ tsp. cinnamon
1$\frac{1}{2}$ cups apple juice

2 eggs, slightly beaten
1 Tbsp. baking powder
$\frac{1}{4}$ tsp. salt
1 cup rolled oats

Mix ingredients together in order given. Pour batter onto preheated, lightly greased waffle iron. Serve warm with Blueberry Topping or ice cream.   4 - 6 servings

BUCKWHEAT PANCAKES

1 cup buckwheat flour
$\frac{1}{2}$ tsp. salt
1 cup apple juice

1 tsp. baking powder
1 egg, beaten
2 Tbsp. olive oil

Beat all ingredients well. Pour onto hot greased pan. Turn pancakes once.   8 - 10 pancakes

OATMEAL PANCAKES

2 cups apple juice
1$\frac{1}{2}$ cups rolled oats
2$\frac{1}{2}$ tsp. baking powder
$\frac{1}{3}$ cup olive oil

2 eggs, beaten
1 cup whole grain flour
1 tsp. salt

Pour juice over oats; allow to soak 5 minutes. Mix rest of ingredients, adding oats last. Pour batter onto hot greased pan (approx. $\frac{1}{4}$ cup per pancake). Turn once. These are good alone or with Pancake Syrup.

12 - 14 pancakes

BLUEBERRY TOPPING For pancakes or waffles

1 qt. blueberries,
    fresh or frozen
3 Tbsp. cornstarch
1 pinch salt

1/4 cup water
1 cup white grape juice
1/2 tsp. lemon juice
1/4 tsp. cinnamon

Stir cornstarch into cup of juice. Meanwhile, in 1 1/2 qt. saucepan, bring blueberries and water to a boil. Stir cornstarch mixture into blueberries. Boil for 2 minutes, stirring constantly. Add rest of ingredients. Serve hot over pancakes and waffles.

PANCAKE SYRUP

6 oz. can frozen apple juice or white grape juice concentrate

1/8 tsp. maple extract
1 pinch salt

1 cup water
1 Tbsp. cornstarch

Mix cornstarch and salt in 1/2 cup cold water. In saucepan bring juice concentrate and 1/2 cup water to a boil. Stir in cornstarch mixture. Stir constantly, allow to boil a few minutes. Remove from heat. Add maple extract. Serve warm.

DATE SYRUP
For date lovers!
6 oz. can white grape juice concentrate

1/4 cup water
1 tsp. cornstarch

1 cup dates
1/4 tsp. vanilla

In saucepan, heat juice concentrate and dates for 5 minutes. Pour into blender. Mix on high until dates are pureed. Return to pan. Dissolve cornstarch in water and stir into fruit. Heat until thickened, stirring constantly. Add vanilla. Serve warm on pancakes, waffles, or ice cream. Also good on zucchini bread.

Hint:
Raspberry bushes have more to offer than fruit! Pick the leaves while they are nice and green. Dry or freeze. Enjoy a warm cup of tea in winter.

BASIC CAROB SYRUP

1½ cups water   1 cup carob powder, sift if lumpy
½ cup smooth peanut butter   4 tsp. vanilla

In saucepan mix water and carob powder and bring to a boil over very slow heat, stirring constantly until syrup is smooth. Add vanilla. Put peanut butter in a small bowl and gradually stir in hot carob mix. Cool and store in refrigerator.

When a recipe calls for melted butter or unsweetened chocolate, the basic carob syrup may be substituted. For semisweet chocolate, add ¼ cup barley malt or 1 tsp. stevia to the basic carob syrup recipe.

This is also a good ice cream topping. Sprinkle chopped nuts over all.

HOT CAROB DRINK

Heat milk. Add basic carob syrup to your taste (approx. 2 Tbsp. to 1 cup of milk).

EGGNOG

Blend together in blender:
1 cup milk   1 egg
1 tsp. vanilla   1 Tbsp. orange juice concentrate
1 pinch salt   ⅛ tsp. cinnamon
dash nutmeg

GRAPE PUNCH

1 qt. grape juice   1 - 12 oz. can orange juice conc.
¼ cup lemon juice
½ cup cranberry juice, unsweetened, opt.

Fill with water to 1 gallon. Drink lots if you have a cold or flu.

Hint: A good natural sweetener for tea is stevia, found in health food stores. Brew stevia leaves with tea leaves.

ICED TEA

Bring water to a boil. Add fresh green tea leaves for twice the desired strength. Cover and remove from heat. Allow to steep for only 5 minutes. Strain into a container almost full of ice. Ice should be almost the same amount as the water you boiled.

Breads

100%
Whole
Grain

POTATO BISCUITS

(Excellent way to use leftover mashed potatoes)

1½ cups mashed potatoes
2 cups whole grain flour
2 tsp. baking soda
½ tsp. cream of tartar
¼ tsp. salt
3 Tbsp. olive oil
1½ cups water

   Beat mashed potatoes to get lumps out. Add rest of ingredients. Mix just until flour disappears. Drop by spoonfuls on cookie sheet. Bake 450° F. for 20 minutes.

QUICK DROP BISCUITS

2 cups whole grain flour
4 tsp. baking powder
1 rounded Tbsp. mayonnaise
⅛ tsp. salt
2 Tbsp. olive oil
⅞ cup milk or apple juice

   Mix just until flour disappears.
Immediately drop by spoonful on cookie sheet.
Bake 375° F. for 10 minutes.
Serve with creamed chicken, apple butter, or jam.

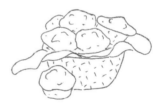

BANANA NUT MUFFINS

In mixer bowl, beat:

2 eggs
⅓ cup butter, melted
2 Tbsp. barley malt or ½ tsp. stevia, opt.
2 ripe bananas
¼ cup apple juice conc.

Add:

2 cups whole grain flour
1 tsp. cinnamon
½ cup chopped nuts
1 Tbsp. baking powder
¼ tsp. salt

   Fill greased muffin tins ¾ full. Bake 20 - 25 minutes at 350° F.
                                    Yield: 15 - 18 muffins

REFRIGERATOR BRAN MUFFINS

Hint:
Whole grain flour may vary. You may need only ⅞ cup per cup of white flour when converting a recipe.

Combine in order given:

3 eggs
1 cup olive oil
1 cup barley malt
     (or) 2 tsp. stevia, opt.
2½ tsp. baking powder
2 Tbsp. baking soda dissolved in
     ¼ cup boiling water

4 cups whole grain flour
3 cups oat bran
1½ Tbsp. molasses
3 cups buttermilk
     (or) apple juice
1 cup raisins

Fill greased muffin cups ⅔ full.
Bake at 375° F. for 20 - 25 minutes.

Note: Batter will keep in refrigerator up to 3 weeks.

APPLE MUFFINS

2 eggs
½ cup applesauce
¼ cup olive oil
½ cup apple juice
¾ tsp. cinnamon
½ tsp. salt

¼ cup oat bran
1¾ cups whole grain flour
2 tsp. baking soda
1 tsp. cream of tartar
¼ tsp. nutmeg
1 cup chopped apples

Beat liquid ingredients together. Add dry ingredients.
Mix until just moistened. Fold apples in.
Fill greased muffin tins ⅔ full.
Bake 400° F. for 20 minutes.

BLUEBERRY MUFFINS

Beat together:
1 cup milk or fruit juice   1 egg
2 Tbsp. olive oil

Add:
2 cups whole grain flour   2 tsp. baking soda
1/2 tsp. salt   1 tsp. cream of tartar
1 tsp. cinnamon   1/4 tsp. nutmeg, opt.
2 Tbsp. barley malt or 1 tsp. stevia, opt.

Mix until just moistened.

Fold in:
1 cup blueberries

Fill greased muffin tins 2/3 full.
Bake 400° F. for 20 - 25 minutes. Remove from pan immediately.

Yield: 1 dozen

> **Tip:**
> Unbleached white flour has the bran and wheat germ removed. While you are making the transition from white to whole grain flour, you may want to substitute part white for a while until you become accustomed to the different texture and flavor.

PUMPKIN MUFFINS

3 Tbsp. fruit juice   1 egg
1/4 cup prunes   3/4 cup canned pumpkin
2 cups whole grain flour   2 tsp. baking soda
1 tsp. cream of tartar   1/2 tsp. salt
1 1/2 tsp. cinnamon   1/4 tsp. ginger
1/4 tsp. nutmeg   1/3 cup apple or prune juice
1/2 cup raisins

Puree juice, egg, and prunes in blender. Pour into mixer bowl and combine rest of ingredients in order given.
Fill greased muffin tins 2/3 full. Sprinkle chopped walnuts on top.
Bake 375° F. for 20 - 25 minutes.

Yield: 1 dozen

RHUBARB MUFFINS

Beat:

2 eggs   4 Tbsp. olive oil

1½ cups milk or apple juice

Add:

3 cups flour   ¾ tsp. salt

2 Tbsp. baking powder   1½ cups fresh rhubarb

1 Tbsp. barley malt or ½ tsp. stevia, opt.   or any fresh fruit

Mix very little. It should be rough and lumpy.

Pour into greased muffin tins. Bake 375° F. for 20 to 25 minutes.

Yield: 2 dozen

CORNBREAD

Beat:

2 eggs   1 cup apple juice

¼ cup olive oil

Add:

1 cup whole grain flour   1 cup yellow cornmeal

dash salt   4 tsp. baking powder

½ tsp. stevia, opt.

Mix only until well blended. Pour into well greased 8 x 12" pan. Bake 400° F. for 30 minutes.

Serve with applesauce, fruit, or fruit juice.

APPLE CORNBREAD

Beat:

2 Tbsp. olive oil   1 egg

Add:

¾ cup cornmeal   ¾ cup whole grain flour

1 Tbsp. baking powder   ½ tsp. salt

¾ cup apple juice   ¾ cup diced apples

Mix until just well blended. Pour into well greased 9 x 9" pan. Bake 400° F. for 25 - 30 minutes.

PUMPKIN CORNBREAD

¾ cup cornmeal
2 Tbsp. barley malt or ½ tsp. stevia, opt.
1 tsp. cinnamon
⅛ tsp. ginger
⅛ tsp. salt
1 cup pumpkin, cooked or canned

1 cup whole grain flour
2 tsp. baking powder
⅛ tsp. nutmeg
⅛ tsp. ground cloves
1 egg
½ cup apple juice

Hint:
For a milder pumpkin taste you can substitute butternut squash in any recipe calling for pumpkin.

Mix all ingredients. Beat until well blended. Pour into a greased 9" loaf pan.
Bake 350° F. for 45 minutes.   Yield: 12 servings

BANANA BREAD

Process in blender:
4 eggs   ½ cup prunes

Pour into mixing bowl.

Add:
1 stick butter, melted   2 tsp. vanilla
4 cups whole grain flour   6 large bananas, mashed
1 tsp. salt   1 cup walnuts, chopped
2 tsp. baking soda

Put into 2 greased loaf pans.
Bake 350° F. 50 - 60 minutes.

BANANA DATE BREAD

Beat:
¼ cup olive oil   1½ cups mashed bananas
1 egg

Mix in:
1¼ cups whole grain flour   ½ tsp. salt
2 tsp. baking powder   1 tsp. baking soda
1 tsp. vanilla
2 Tbsp. apple or white grape juice concentrate

Stir in:
1 cup dates   ½ cup chopped nuts

Pour into a greased loaf pan.
Bake 350° F. for 1 hour.   Cool before cutting.

100%
Whole
Grain

CAROB CHIP PUMPKIN BREAD

Cream:

$2/3$ cup prune butter, or blended prunes

$1\frac{1}{2}$ cups canned pumpkin
3 eggs

Add:

$2\frac{1}{3}$ cups whole grain flour
2 tsp. baking soda
1 tsp. salt

$\frac{1}{2}$ cup apple juice
1 tsp. cinnamon
$\frac{1}{2}$ tsp. cloves

Fold in:

$1\frac{1}{2}$ cups carob chips

Pour into 2 greased loaf pans. Bake at 350° F. for 45 minutes.

SWEET POTATO BREAD

(Good way to use up those tiny sweet potatoes.)

4 eggs
$2/3$ cup olive oil
$2/3$ cup fruit juice
4 cups cooked mashed sweet potatoes
$3\frac{1}{3}$ cups whole grain flour
$\frac{1}{2}$ tsp. baking powder

2 tsp. baking soda
1 tsp. cinnamon
1 tsp. nutmeg
$\frac{1}{2}$ tsp. ginger
$2/3$ cup raisins
$2/3$ cup chopped nuts

Beat wet ingredients together. Add rest of ingredients and mix. Bake 70 minutes at 350° F. Cool before removing from pan.

ZUCCHINI BREAD

Mix well:

3 eggs
$\frac{1}{2}$ cup barley malt or 1 tsp. stevia

1 cup olive oil
2 tsp. vanilla

Add and mix:

$1\frac{1}{2}$ tsp. baking soda
3 cups whole grain flour
$\frac{1}{4}$ tsp. nutmeg

$3/4$ tsp. baking powder
2 tsp. cinnamon

Stir in:

2 cups shredded zucchini (not peeled)
1 cup chopped nuts

1 cup raisins

Divide in 2 small or 1 large greased loaf pan. Bake 350° F. for 1 hour.

OATMEAL BREAD

YEAST BREAD TIPS
ON PAGE 22.

2 cups boiling white grape juice poured over:

1 cup rolled oats $^1/_2$ cup whole grain flour

Stir in:

1 Tbsp. salt   2 Tbsp. butter
3 Tbsp. vinegar   1 Tbsp. lecithin, opt.

    Let stand until lukewarm.

Dissolve:

2 Tbsp. yeast in:
$^1/_2$ cup warm water

Add to batter and knead with:

5 - 6 cups whole grain flour

    Let rise, covered, for 1 hour. Punch down. Allow to rise another 30 minutes. Work out into 2 loaves. Place in greased pans. Allow to rise about $^1/_2$ hour.
Bake 350° F. for 35 minutes.

OAT BRAN BREAD

$2^1/_2$ cups white grape juice   5 - 6 cups whole grain flour
2 Tbsp. yeast   1 cup oat bran
2 Tbsp. butter   2 Tbsp. vinegar
1 Tbsp. salt   2 Tbsp. lecithin, opt.

    In mixer bowl, sprinkle yeast over warm juice. When it is frothy add the rest of the ingredients except 3 cups of the flour and the bran.   Beat until smooth. Gradually add 3 cups flour, bran, and additional flour if needed. This dough should be a little sticky to touch as it tends to be a dry bread. Allow to rise 1 - 1$^1/_2$ hours. Work out into 2 loaves. Place in greased pans. Cover and allow to rise $^1/_2$ hour. Bake 350° F. for 40 minutes.

For variety, add:

$^3/_4$ cup raisins
1 tsp. cinnamon

WHOLE GRAIN BREAD

Lecithin in the diet helps to keep the body from building up cholesterol, and also helps to lower it if you already have cholesterol.

Lecithin makes baked goods less crumbly. Lecithin is a soy product.

2³/₄ cups warm white grape juice or apple juice
2 Tbsp. dry yeast
¹/₄ cup instant mashed potato flakes
     (or) 1 cup leftover mashed potatoes
1 Tbsp. lecithin, opt.   2 tsp. salt
¹/₄ cup olive oil   6 cups spelt flour
4 Tbsp. vinegar   2 - 2¹/₂ cups spelt flour

Dissolve yeast in warm juice. While beating with mixer at medium speed, gradually add remaining ingredients except for 2 cups of flour. Work in the rest of the flour until it doesn't feel sticky to the touch.   Knead 5 - 10 minutes. Let rise covered 1 hour.
Work out into loaves, place in greased pans, and prick all the way through with a fork. Cover and allow to rise ¹/₂ hour.
Bake for 30 minutes at 350° F.

Note: If your bread pans are big, make a double batch and work into 5 loaves.   Yield: 3 loaves

DATE NUT BREAD

(Delicious!)

2¹/₄ cups warm white grape juice
2 Tbsp. yeast
2 tsp. salt   2 Tbsp. vinegar
1 Tbsp. lecithin, opt.   3 cups whole grain flour
¹/₂ cup pecans, chopped   1 cup chopped dates
3 - 4 cups whole grain flour   1 tsp. cinnamon

In mixer bowl, sprinkle yeast over warm juice.
When it is frothy add the rest of the ingredients except 3 - 4 cups flour. Beat until smooth. Gradually add remaining flour until not sticky to touch. Knead 5 - 10 minutes. Allow to rise covered, 1 - 1¹/₂ hours.
Work out into 2 - 3 loaves. Place in greased pans, cover and allow to rise ¹/₂ hour.
Bake 375° F. for 30 - 40 minutes.

BUTTERHORNS

In mixer bowl, mix together and let set a few minutes:
3 Tbsp. frozen grape juice concentrate in measuring cup, filling to 1 cup
with hot water (Mixture should be lukewarm)
1 Tbsp. yeast
$\frac{1}{2}$ tsp. salt

Then add:

$\frac{1}{2}$ cup melted butter   3 eggs
2 tsp. vinegar   4$\frac{1}{4}$ cups whole grain flour

   Mix and cover with plastic wrap. Refrigerate several hours or overnight.
Grease muffin tins and place 2 walnut size balls of dough in each cup.
Let rise at room temperature for 2 - 4 hours.
Bake 375° F. for 10 - 12 minutes.

Note: For guests, I use 1 cup whole grain and 3$\frac{1}{4}$ cups all purpose flour.
                                    Makes 2 dozen

YEAST BREAD TIPS
ON PAGE 22.

CINNAMON ROLLS

1 cup warm white grape juice   1$\frac{1}{2}$ tsp. salt
1 Tbsp. yeast   2 eggs
$\frac{1}{3}$ cup olive oil   1 tsp. vinegar
1$\frac{1}{2}$ cups whole grain flour   2$\frac{1}{2}$ - 3 cups whole grain flour
$\frac{1}{2}$ tsp. lemon juice

   Sprinkle yeast over juice. Allow to soak.
Add all ingredients except the last 2$\frac{1}{2}$ - 3 cups flour, and beat together.
Gradually add remaining flour. Knead 3 - 5 minutes.
Let rise in warm place about 1$\frac{1}{2}$ hours.

Roll dough out and spread with:

Option 1: melted butter   **Option 2:** melted butter
        cinnamon   1 shredded apple
        chopped walnuts $\frac{1}{2}$ - 1 cup raisins
        date sugar

   Press slightly into dough. Roll up like a jelly roll and slice in 1" slices.
Place in greased baking pan. Let rise 1 hour.
Bake 350° F. for 30 - 40 minutes.

Tips for Better Whole Grain Yeast Breads

For sugar free yeast breads:
        Use 1 tsp. apple juice concentrate for each Tbsp. of yeast used.   The natural sugars in the juice makes the yeast "work".

 When using fruit juice in bread, it rises better if the juice contains ascorbic acid, resulting in a lighter bread.

When baking bread have all the ingredients room temperature except the yeast. Dissolve yeast in water that is 105 - 115° F.

It is important that yeast is allowed time to dissolve and grow in warm juice - allow 5 minutes. It should appear light and spongy. If it doesn't, then start over again.

Grinding your own flour produces a tastier, more nutritious product, but a heavier bread. Allow 1 extra rising.

Wheat germ is a good source of vitamin E. Replace 1 Tbsp. flour per cup with wheat germ.

Want a lighter bread? Do not "dump" flour in by cupfuls, but slowly add flour to yeast bread as you knead the bread, which results in a lighter bread.

Do not allow yeast bread to rise too long or it will result in a heavy bread.

Remove yeast breads from pans immediately after baking. Cover with a towel, and cool before storing in plastic bags, or it will become wet and soggy.

Allow yeast bread to cool before slicing, or it may fall and seem under baked.

Main Dishes

BAKED BEANS

1 lb. ground beef
1 large onion
5 cups beans, cooked and drained (kidney, pinto, etc. mixed)
2 tsp. vinegar
1½ cups ketchup
⅛ - ¼ cup barley malt or 1 tsp. stevia
2 Tbsp. mustard

Brown meat and onion. Stir in remaining ingredients. Pour into casserole.
Bake at 400° F. for 30 - 35 minutes, until hot and bubbly.

Note: Dried beans should be soaked overnight, then cooked until soft, about 1 hour.

8 - 12 servings

Forget to soak your dry beans overnight?

Cover the beans with water. Bring to a boil. Remove from heat. Let set 1 - 1½ hours. Drain soak water. Add fresh water to cover beans. Cook 1 - 1½ hours until soft.

Changing the soak water helps to make the beans less "gassy".

BEEF AND POTATO LOAF

Prepare:
4 cups thinly sliced or french-fry cut potatoes

Spread an even layer in a greased two qt. casserole, alternating with next layer.

Layer between potatoes:
1 Tbsp. chopped onion
½ tsp. salt
1 tsp. parsley flakes
½ tsp. pepper

Combine, then spread on potatoes:
1 lb. ground beef
½ cup rolled oats
¾ cup tomato juice or ketchup

Spread additional ketchup on meatloaf. Bake at 350° F. for 1 to 1½ hours or until potatoes are tender.

6 - 8 servings

BEEF PINWHEELS

Mix together:

1 lb. ground beef or
    ground turkey
1/2 tsp. salt
1/8 tsp. garlic powder
1 egg, well beaten

2 tsp. chicken seasoning
1 small onion, diced
1/8 tsp. black pepper
1/3 cup fine, dry bread crumbs
2 Tbsp. tomato juice or ketchup

Roll out on Saran Wrap, 12 x 8 x 1/2" thick. Spread 1 1/2 cups cooled mashed potatoes on 1/2 of rectangle. Spread 1 pt. cooked mashed peas on other half. Roll up. Place in pan. Spread ketchup on top. Bake uncovered at 350° F. for 1 - 1 1/4 hours.

Note: If making a double batch, roll up in two rolls. Place side by side in cake pan.

Hint:

Broccoli stems can be mixed with the florets. First slice stems diagonally, then cut in small pieces.

BROCCOLI RICE CASSEROLE

4 cups chicken broth
2 cups brown rice, uncooked
2 cups fresh broccoli,
    chopped and steamed

2 cups water
1/2 tsp. salt
1 pt. chicken, cooked, chopped
1 tsp. chicken seasoning

Simmer all ingredients except broccoli for 1 - 1 1/2 hours. Add broccoli just before serving.

Optional: To serve, melt Velveeta cheese over top.

CABBAGE - RICE CASSEROLE

1 lb. ground beef
1/2 tsp. salt
1/3 cup brown rice, uncooked
1 small head cabbage, chopped

1 small onion, chopped
1 tsp. chicken seasoning
2 1/4 cups tomato juice

Brown meat in large kettle. Add onion and seasonings. Add rice, then pour juice over. Top with cabbage. Do not stir. Simmer 1 1/2 hours.

CHICKEN POTATO DUMPLINGS

Place in 2¹/₂ qt. casserole in order given:

5 - 6 cooked potatoes,   1 pint cooked peas
      diced or sliced

Bring to a boil:

2 cups cooked chicken   2 cups chicken broth
1 tsp. salt   ¹/₈ tsp. pepper
3 Tbsp. whole grain flour
   Pour over vegetables and top with biscuit batter.

Biscuits:

1¹/₂ cups whole grain flour   1 Tbsp. baking powder
¹/₈ tsp. salt   2 Tbsp. olive oil
²/₃ cup milk or apple juice

   Bake uncovered at 375° F. for 20 - 25 minutes or until biscuits are done. Bake 15 - 20 minutes longer if all your ingredients aren't hot before adding the biscuits.   Serves 6 - 8

CHICKEN POTPIE

1 pie crust   1 cup cooked chicken pieces
3 cups vegetables, cooked and bite sized (potatoes, carrots,
              celery, peas, green beans, etc.)

   Use leftover gravy, Cream Soup (page 61), or combine 1¹/₂ cups cold tomato juice and 2 Tbsp. cornstarch. Cook over medium heat, stirring constantly. Salt and pepper to taste.

Variation: Brown ¹/₂ lb. ground beef and onion, minced. Stir in 4 Tbsp. flour, then 1¹/₂ cups tomato juice. Add vegetables. Pour into pie crust. Top with crust or biscuits. Make slits in crust.

   Bake at 375° F. for 40 minutes. If filling is cold, bake 10 - 15 minutes longer or until bubbly.

Spiritual nugget:
   Those who see God's hand in everything......
   are content to leave everything in God's hand!

CHICKEN RICE CASSEROLE

Hint:
    Use brown rice. White rice has had many valuable nutrients removed.

Bring to a boil:
1 qt. broth

Stir in:
1/3 cup whole grain flour

Stir while boiling for 2 minutes.

Mix thickened broth with:

1 pt. cooked chicken or turkey 1 tsp. soy sauce
1 cup water 1 cup brown rice, uncooked
3/4 cup chopped celery 1 Tbsp. melted butter
1 chopped onion salt and pepper

Pour into greased casserole; cover and bake at 350° F. for 1 1/2 hours.

CHICKEN RICE DELUXE

2 cups cooked chicken, 1 1/2 cups chopped celery
       chopped 1/3 cup chopped green pepper
1 chopped onion 3 cups cooked brown rice
2 cups Cream Soup 1 tsp. salt
     (page 61) 2 Tbsp. lemon juice
1 1/2 cups mayonnaise mixed 5 hard boiled eggs, diced
   with 1/2 cup broth or water

Mix all ingredients. Bake 1 hour in 2 1/2 qt. casserole at 350° F.

6 - 8 servings

DRESSING

1 Tbsp. butter or olive oil 10 slices of bread (about 6 c.)
2 stalks celery, chopped 1 med. onion, chopped
2 tsp. sage salt and pepper to taste
4 oz. can mushrooms, broth, 1 - 2 cups
     undrained

Toast bread and tear or cut into small pieces. Saute celery and onions in butter or oil. Mix all ingredients together, adding broth until just moistened if stuffing turkey. If baking in casserole, add more broth and 3 Tbsp. butter.
Bake covered at 350° F. for 1/2 hour, then uncovered for 1/2 hour.

HAMBURGER RICE CASSEROLE

6 cups broth
1 tsp. salt
2 cups brown rice, uncooked
1 lb. ground beef
1 small onion, chopped
1/4 cup whole grain flour
1 1/2 cups water

1 cup celery, diced and
                cooked
1 - 4 oz. can mushrooms,
              chopped fine
1 Tbsp. instant chicken
             seasoning

> **MSG -** (Monosodium Glutamate) It is an additive often found in canned soups, chicken and beef broths, as well as in other canned foods. Some individuals are highly sensitive to it. *(See section in back of book for more on MSG)*

   Simmer broth, salt and rice 1 hour or until soft.
Meanwhile, brown meat and onion. Stir in flour.
Add water, stirring constantly until thickened.
Add mushrooms, celery and chicken seasoning.
Stir into rice after rice is done.
Serve immediately or pour into casserole and refrigerate until needed.
Bake at 350° F. for 1 hour.

EGG FU YUNG

In blender, mix:
8 eggs
1/4 cup onions
1/2 cup celery
salt and pepper

1 cup cooked chicken pieces
1/4 cup mushrooms
1 Tbsp. whole grain flour

In greased skillet, fry mixture in:
patties until brown on both sides.
Serve over rice.
Top with gravy.

Gravy:
3 cups chicken broth, boiling

Stir into broth: 4 Tbsp. clear jel or cornstarch dissolved in 1/4 cup water
Boil, stirring constantly, for 1 minute.
Add salt and pepper to taste.

Serves 4 - 6

EGGPLANT CASSEROLE

Saute:

2 Tbsp. butter   3 Tbsp. finely chopped onion

Add:

1 lb. ground beef, brown until done

Add:

3 ripe peeled tomatoes, cut up
salt and pepper to taste

  Simmer 20 minutes.

Add:

1 tsp. parsley (optional)   ¹/₄ tsp. minced garlic or dash
                                    of powdered garlic

Saute:

3 diced eggplants in butter until browned

SAUCE

Melt:

2 Tbsp. butter in small pan

Add:

1 Tbsp. whole grain flour, rounded

Gradually add:

1 cup broth or milk

  Bring to boil.

Add:

¹/₂ cup grated cheese

  Simmer until cheese is melted.

Cover bottom of greased casserole with layer of eggplant, then layer of meat. Continue layering, ending with eggplant layer on top. Pour cheese sauce on. Sprinkle on additional cheese or Velveeta slices and ¹/₂ cup buttered bread crumbs.
Brown in hot oven at 400° F.

Serves 8

Tip: Peeling tomatoes?

Place tomatoes in boiling water for 1 minute, then plunge into cold water. Skins will slip right off.

HOBOS

Divide following ingredients in order given on 10 pieces of foil, shiny side up:

1 small head cabbage, finely sliced (reserve half)
3 sliced potatoes, need not be peeled
3 sliced carrots
1½ lb. ground beef, formed into 10 patties
sliced onions
catsup
slice of Velveeta, optional
cabbage, sliced
salt and pepper to taste

Seal foil tightly. Bake in 350° F. oven for 1 hour or put on hot charcoal or hot coals and cook 12 minutes on each side.

LENTIL RICE CASSEROLE

4 cups chicken broth
½ tsp. salt
¾ cup chopped onion
¼ tsp. oregano
⅛ tsp. garlic powder

1 cup lentils, uncooked
¾ cup brown rice, uncooked
½ tsp. basil
¼ tsp. thyme

Blend all together in casserole.
Bake, covered, at 300° F. for 1½ hours.

Optional: Top with ½ cup cheese last 20 minutes.

LENTILS

1 qt. chicken broth
1 lb. ground beef, browned
1 stalk celery, chopped fine
1 Tbsp. chicken seasoning

1 qt. water
1 small onion, diced
1 tsp. salt
1 lb. lentils

Bring water and broth to a boil. Add rest of ingredients. Simmer for 1 hour.

How about a meatless meal? Try using beans, lentils, split peas, and nuts for part of your protein needs, since too much animal proteins bogs down the kidneys and liver.

Meats also create an acid condition in the body.

It is believed that most Americans eat too much protein. The need varies, depending on our physical build and also activity factors, with 60 - 80 grams daily being the requirement for most people.

QUICK LENTILS

4¹/₂ cups water
¹/₂ stalk celery, diced
1 small onion, chopped
1 tsp. salt

2 cups lentils
1 medium carrot, diced
1 Tbsp. chicken seasoning
¹/₈ tsp. oregano

Mix all ingredients in kettle.
Simmer covered until soft, 40 - 45 minutes.

8 - 10 servings

Time Saver: When browning ground beef, do as much as will fit into your skillet. Take out the extra and freeze it in pint boxes for quick casserole preparation later.

MEATBALL STEW

In large kettle:

5 medium potatoes, diced
4 carrots, sliced

1 onion, chopped

Simmer covered 45 minutes or until done.

Meanwhile combine:

1¹/₂ lbs. ground beef
1 tsp. salt
1 cup bread crumbs

¹/₄ cup chopped onion
¹/₄ tsp. thyme
1 egg, beaten

Brown meatballs. Dump onto top of vegetables. Make a gravy from brownings. To gravy add 1 Tbsp. instant chicken seasoning, 4 oz. can mushrooms and salt. Pour over all.

8 - 10 servings

MEXICAN CHILI PIE

Brown:

1 lb. ground beef

1 medium onion

Stir 2 Tbsp. whole grain flour into browned meat. Stir 15 oz. tomato juice into meat. Bring to a boil and stir 2 minutes.

Add:

1 cup kidney beans
¹/₈ tsp. garlic salt
1 - 2 tsp. chili powder
¹/₄ tsp. cumin
¹/₄ cup diced green pepper

¹/₄ tsp. oregano
¹/₈ tsp. salt
1 tsp. dry mustard
pinch red pepper

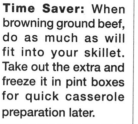

Pour into 8 x 12" pan.

(see following page for topping)

32

TOPPING:

3/4 cup cornmeal
1/2 cup whole grain flour
1/2 tsp. baking soda
1/2 tsp. salt
1 cup (4 oz.) shredded cheddar cheese (optional)
3/4 cup buttermilk or fruit juice
1 egg, lightly beaten
2 Tbsp. olive oil

Time Saver: When you are using a tried and proven yummy recipe, make a double batch. Freeze half for those busy days when you don't have time to bake or cook.

Combine dry ingredients.
Combine the rest and stir into dry ingredients, just until moistened.
Spread over filling.
Bake at 450° F. for 15 minutes.

MEXICAN CASSEROLE

Biscuit Crust:

2 cups whole grain flour
1/8 tsp. salt
2 Tbsp. olive oil

4 tsp. baking powder
1 rounded Tbsp. mayonnaise
7/8 cup apple juice

Pat into greased 9 x13" pan.
Bake at 375° F. for 10 minutes.

Brown:

1 1/2 lb. ground beef

1 small onion

Add:

2 cups pizza sauce
1/4 tsp. garlic powder

1/2 tsp. oregano

Mix and pour on crust.

Top with:

1 cup sour cream

1 cup shredded cheddar cheese

Bake at 350° F. for 30 minutes.

Top with chopped fresh tomatoes.

8 servings

MEXICAN DISH

Cook:

4½ cups water

1½ cups brown rice

1 tsp. salt

Brown:

1 lb. ground beef

1 medium onion

Add:

2 cups pizza sauce

2 Tbsp. diced peppers

1 tsp. chili powder

1 can mushrooms

1½ tsp. chicken seasoning

Mix with rice. Put in casserole. Top with 1 bag finely crushed corn chips. Place Velveeta cheese slices on top. Bake at 325° F. for 30 minutes.

Serves 10 - 12

MIXED VEGGIE BAKE

Biscuit Crust:

2 cups whole grain flour

⅛ tsp. salt

2 Tbsp. olive oil

4 tsp. baking powder

1 rounded Tbsp. mayonnaise

⅞ cup milk or apple juice

Mix and spread in greased 9 x 13" pan.
Prebake at 375° F. for 10 - 12 minutes.

1 lb. ground beef

½ cup chopped onion

2 cups Cream Soup (page 61)

1½ cups Velveeta or cheddar cheese

2 cups frozen mixed vegetables (or make your own mixture)

Brown ground beef and onion. Melt cheese into meat and stir cream soup into it. Spread vegetables on top of biscuit crust, then meat mixture. Bake at 350° F. for 30 minutes.

Note: If you don't have cream soup made ahead, omit soup. Add 3 Tbsp. flour to browned meat. Stir 2 cups milk or broth into meat. Bring to a boil and add cheese and ½ tsp. salt.

Serves 8

HOMEMADE NOODLES

Beat until very light:
2 eggs or 4 egg yolks   1 Tbsp. olive oil
Beat in $1/4$ cup cold water. $1/2$ tsp. salt

Add, working with hands when dough is too stiff:
2 - $2^{1}/_{2}$ cups whole grain flour

   Dough should be very stiff. Allow dough to rest covered $1/2$ hour. Put through Pasta Maker (or) divide dough in 4 parts. Roll each part out as thin as possible on a lightly floured board. Hang over drying rack and allow to dry $1/2$ - 1 hour. Flour if sticky, then roll up like jelly roll and cut noodles desired width. Spread out to finish drying on counter lightly dusted with cornstarch or flour.

HOMEMADE NOODLES (EGG FREE)

Instead of using eggs, increase water to $1/2$ cup and proceed with above recipe.

EASY HOMEMADE PIZZA

1 Tbsp. dry yeast   1 cup warm water
3 cups whole grain flour $1^{1}/_{2}$ tsp. salt
$1/4$ cup olive oil

   Dissolve yeast in warm water. Add salt and oil and mix thoroughly. Add $1/2$ of flour and beat until no lumps. Gradually add remaining flour. Knead 5 minutes. Press on pizza pan. Let rise 5 - 10 minutes. Prebake crust at 375° F. for 10 minutes. Add toppings. Return to oven for 20 minutes or until cheese is browned.

Note: If you like a thinner crust, make a double batch of crust. Press into 3 pizza pans. Freeze the extra crusts for a quick pizza.

Note: If you like lots of toppings or your pizza sauce is thin, add 2 - 3 Tbsp. flour to your browned meat. Stir pizza sauce in. Cook until thick. Pour on crust and add toppings.

PIZZA CUPS

1 lb. ground beef
2 Tbsp. whole grain flour
1- 4 oz. can mushrooms

1 small onion, minced
2 cups pizza sauce
1 Tbsp. green pepper, diced

Brown meat and onion. Stir in flour and pizza sauce. Bring to a boil, stirring constantly. Remove from heat and add rest of ingredients.

BISCUITS

$2^3/_4$ cups whole grain flour
$1/_8$ tsp. salt
2 Tbsp. olive oil

4 tsp. baking powder
1 rounded Tbsp. mayonnaise
$7/_8$ cup milk or apple juice

Mix until flour disappears. Let set 5 minutes. Press into greased muffin tins, cover bottom and sides. Spoon meat mixture in. Sprinkle with shredded cheddar or mozzarella cheese. Bake at 400° F. for 12 minutes.   Yields 18 pizza cups.

HAYSTACKS

Hint: You can cook rice in the oven: In $2^1/_2$ qt. casserole place: 6 cups water, 2 cups brown rice, and salt. Bake 350° F. for $1^1/_2$ hours.

Place on plate in order given:
3 cups crackers (broken coarsely)
6 cups brown rice, cooked
1 head lettuce, shredded
3 tomatoes, diced
2 lb. ground beef, browned, with 1 qt. pizza sauce added
9 oz. corn chips, crushed
onions, chopped

CHEESE SAUCE

Bring $1/_2$ cup water to a boil in skillet.
Stir in 3 Tbsp. whole grain flour mixed with 1 cup milk.
Bring to a boil, stirring constantly.
Add 1 Tbsp. diced green pepper, $1/_2$ tsp. chili powder, $1/_2$ tsp. paprika, pinch salt and 1 lb. Velveeta cheese.
Add milk if too thick.

Top with:
chopped peanuts

Serves 8

POTATO BAR

Place on plate in order given:
12 baked potatoes
2 lb. ground beef, browned, and 1 qt. pizza sauce added
sour cream or yogurt
1 lb. shredded cheddar cheese
onions, chopped
2 - 4 oz. cans mushrooms
cheese sauce *(see Haystacks)*

Meat can be done ahead and warmed up in crockpot.
Make cheese sauce just before serving.   Serves 8 - 12

Time and Penny Saver: To prevent many trips to the grocery store, keep a list handy in the kitchen to list items as you think of them. This also prevents a lot of impulse buying.

POTATO BEEF CASSEROLE

2 cups broth
2 stalks celery, chunked
1 large onion, sliced
1 - 4 oz. can mushrooms
$1/2$ tsp. salt
$1/8$ tsp. pepper
1 lb. ground beef, browned
5 - 6 med. potatoes, sliced or diced

In skillet, simmer broth, celery, onion and mushrooms for 20 min. Meanwhile, place meat and uncooked potatoes in $2^1/2$ qt. casserole.
Liquify broth and vegetables in blender.
Pour into potatoes and stir together.
Bake, covered, at 350° F. for 1 hour.
Remove lid and bake an additional 15 - 30 min.

POTATO LASAGNA

Your guests will love this!

3 large potatoes, cooked and thinly sliced

Brown:
1 lb. ground beef

Add:
1 med. onion
$^1/_8$ tsp. oregano
dash garlic powder

1 tsp. salt
$^1/_4$ tsp. pepper
1$^1/_2$ cups pizza sauce

Combine:
1 egg
$^1/_2$ cup shredded mozzarella cheese

1 cup cottage cheese

Arrange $^1/_2$ of potato slices in greased 2$^1/_2$ qt. casserole. Spread $^1/_2$ of cottage cheese mixture on, then thin slices of Velveeta. Then $^1/_2$ of meat mixture. Repeat layers, omitting Velveeta cheese.
Bake at 350° F. for 1 hour.
Can be put together the day before and refrigerated.

Serves 8 - 10

RICE AND CURRY

Saute:
1$^1/_2$ tsp. curry powder
$^1/_4$ cup minced onion

3 Tbsp. butter

Add:
3 Tbsp. whole grain flour
$^3/_4$ tsp. salt
   Cook until bubbly.

1 cup broth
1 cup milk or water

Add:
1 lb. ground beef, browned
$^1/_2$ tsp. lemon juice

   Boil 1 minute.

Serve over rice with the following toppings:

diced bananas
diced hard boiled eggs
diced onions
chopped tomato
crushed pineapple

chopped peanuts
diced peppers
shredded cheese
coconut
pickles

SHIPWRECK CASSEROLE

¼ cup brown rice, uncooked
4 cups raw potatoes, sliced
1 lb. ground beef, browned
1½ cups tomato juice
2 cups kidney beans
1 large onion, chopped

1 stalk celery, diced
½ cup water
1 Tbsp. butter, melted
1 tsp. salt
¼ tsp. pepper

> **Hint: Cooking dried beans?**
> Add salt after cooking. If salt is added during cooking, it slows down the cooking process.

Put rice in bottom of greased casserole. Mix rest of ingredients together and pour into casserole. Cover and bake 350° F. for 2 hours. Stir before serving.

Serves 8 - 10

SKILLET TUNA POTATO CASSEROLE

4 medium potatoes, sliced
1 - 6 oz. can tuna, drained
1 - 4 oz. can mushrooms, undrained
Velveeta cheese, optional

In skillet, cook potatoes in 1 - 2 Tbsp. olive oil until just soft. Add rest of ingredients and heat through. If too dry, add ¼ - ½ cup water. Add salt and pepper to taste.

SPANISH RICE

1 lb. ground beef, browned
1 cup brown rice, uncooked
dash pepper

4 cups tomato juice
½ tsp. salt
2 tsp. chili powder

Place rice in bottom of casserole. Add seasonings to ground beef. Put all ingredients in casserole. Do not stir. Bake covered 350° F. for 1½ - 2 hours.

Opt: Melt 2 thick slices Velveeta in before serving.

QUICK GOLDEN STEW

Cook ½ hour:

4 carrots, chunked

2 cups potatoes, diced

1 large onion, diced

1 stalk celery, diced

Add:

1 pint frozen peas

    Do not stir! Cook ½ hour longer.

1 lb. ground beef, browned

Dissolve:

3 Tbsp. cornstarch in ½ cup water

    Add to vegetables, stirring constantly.
Allow to cook 1 - 2 minutes.

Add:

½ - 1 cup milk or water until right consistency.

Add:

salt and pepper to taste.

Opt: 2 slices Velveeta cheese melted in just before serving.

Hint:

    Cover ground beef to brown. Drain fat off.

    Makes kitchen clean-up easier and cuts down on fat intake.

CORN TORTILLAS

1 cup whole grain flour

½ tsp. salt

1½ cups cold water

½ cup cornmeal

2 Tbsp. olive oil

1 egg

    Mix together. Cook in skillet using 3 Tbsp. of the batter per tortilla.

Put on your own toppings:

Browned ground beef with pizza sauce added (should be thick consistency.)

mashed beans

minced onions

salsa

chopped tomatoes

shredded cheese

    We put another tortilla on top, sandwich style.

Makes 1 dozen tortillas

TAMALE PIE

Tamale pie filling:
2 cups canned tomatoes or tomato juice
1 lb. ground beef
1/4 tsp. garlic powder
1 cup chopped onion
1/2 cup chopped celery

2 cups corn
1 tsp. salt
2 tsp. chili powder

Preheat oven to 375° F. Brown meat on medium heat; drain fat. Add remaining ingredients. Simmer uncovered on low heat for 10 minutes.
Line greased 8 x 12" baking pan with 1/2 recipe for cornmeal crust. Add tamale pie filling. Top with remaining cornmeal mixture.
Bake 375° F. for 40 minutes.

Time Saver:
Chop onions and wrap in individual saran wraps or small baggies. Freeze for quick addition to frying meat or casseroles.

Cornmeal crust:

Measure into 1 1/2 qt. saucepan:
1 cup cornmeal
1/2 tsp. salt

1/2 tsp. chili powder

Stir in:
1 3/4 cups milk or water

1 cup water

Cook over low heat, stirring constantly, until mixture becomes very thick.   Serves 6 - 8

TATER TOT CASSEROLE

1 1/2 lb. ground beef
1 egg, slightly beaten
1 small onion
1 tsp. salt
1/8 tsp. pepper

1 pint canned green beans
2 cups Cream Soup with
        mushrooms *(page 61)*
Tater Tots

Mix first five ingredients. Press into 8 x 12" pan. Spread green beans over meat. Pour cream soup over. Place frozen Tater Tots over entire dish.
Bake 350° F. for 1 hour.   Serves 6 - 8

TUNA NOODLE CASSEROLE

Tip: When cooking noodles, bring water to a boil; add noodles, cover and turn heat off. Let set 25 minutes. This prevents boiling over, sticking, and having to watch them.

12 oz. whole grain noodles, uncooked
3 Tbsp. butter
3 Tbsp. whole grain flour
1 cup chicken broth

1 tsp. chicken seasoning
1 - 6 oz. can tuna, drained
1/4 tsp. salt
1 - 4 oz. can mushrooms, undrained

Cook noodles in boiling salted water until barely soft but biteable. Meanwhile melt butter in fry pan. Remove from heat and stir flour in, then broth. Return to heat, stirring constantly, until mixture boils 2 minutes. Stir in rest of ingredients. Drain noodles and mix with tuna and sauce. Pour into casserole. Bake 350° F. for 30 minutes or until hot and bubbly.

TURKEY - A - LA - KING

In large skillet saute:
1 medium onion in 2 Tbsp. butter or olive oil

Add:
2 Tbsp. whole grain flour

Stir in:
2 cups milk or broth
Bring to a boil, stirring constantly 2 - 3 minutes.

Add:
2 cups chopped, cooked turkey
2 Tbsp. diced peppers
1/8 tsp. pepper

1/2 tsp. salt
2 cups peas
mushrooms, opt.

Cook until heated through.

Last few minutes, add:
3 diced hard boiled eggs, opt.

Serve over rice, toast or biscuits.

Note: Chicken may also be used instead of turkey.

TUNA STUFFED POTATOES

Bake uncovered:
4 large potatoes

Cut potatoes in half lengthwise while still hot. Scoop potato out of shells, reserving shells.

Toss scooped out potatoes with:

2 - 6 oz. cans tuna, drained
1/4 cup green peppers
1/4 cup chopped onion

1/2 cup butter
1/2 cup grated cheddar cheese, opt.

> **Time Saver:**
> To save time, when chopping onions, do a few extra. Store in refrigerator in a plastic bag or cottage cheese carton. It will keep up to a week.

Spoon mixture into shells. Bake 400° F. for 20 minutes.

SHEPHERD'S PIE (Excellent way to use up leftover Thanksgiving dinner; turkey and mashed potatoes.)

2 cups roast turkey, chopped (or) 1 lb. ground beef, browned
1 cup fresh mushrooms (or) 1 - 4 oz. can
1 medium onion
3 Tbsp. tomato paste
1 tsp. ground mustard
2 cups mixed vegetables

1 clove garlic
1 cup broth
1 tsp. salt
dash pepper

Saute onion and garlic in olive oil. Mix all ingredients together in casserole.

Top with:
8 medium potatoes, peeled, cooked, and mashed
1 cup cheddar cheese, shredded
2 egg whites, stiffly beaten

Gently fold egg whites into mashed potatoes and cheese. Bake uncovered 425° F. for 15 minutes. Reduce heat to 350° F. for 20 minutes longer or until meat layer is bubbly.

Serves 6 - 8

SPAGHETTI SQUASH SUPREME

1 medium spaghetti squash
1/2 cup water
1 lb. ground beef or sausage
1 clove garlic, minced
2 cups tomatoes, chopped
2 cups pinto, northern, or kidney beans
1/4 tsp. oregano

1 medium onion
1 medium green pepper
dash pepper
1/4 tsp. celery salt
1 tsp. salt
Parmesan cheese, opt.

Cut squash in half lengthwise. Discard seeds. Place cut side down in baking pan. Add water and cover. Bake 350° F. for 1 hour or until just tender.

Meanwhile brown meat. Drain fat off. Add vegetables. Simmer until tender-crisp. Add beans and seasonings. Simmer 10 minutes. Scrape squash out of shell with fork. Mix with meat mixture. Serve with Parmesan cheese if desired.

STIR FRY

Sauce:
2 Tbsp. cornstarch dissolved in 1/4 cup water
1 cup broth
2 Tbsp. soy sauce
1 Tbsp. lemon juice, opt.

In medium saucepan bring broth to a boil. Stir in rest of ingredients.   Boil 1 - 2 minutes, stirring constantly.
Set aside.

Saute in 2 Tbsp. olive oil:
1/2 lb. bite size chicken pieces

Remove chicken.

Saute in 2 Tbsp. olive oil:
4 - 6 cups fresh vegetables, sliced diagonally, bite size (carrots, onion, broccoli, cauliflower, celery, pepper, zucchini, mushrooms, snow peas, mung beans sprouts)

Saute carrots, onions, and cauliflower first. Toss a few minutes and add other vegetables, saving snow peas and sprouts until last. Vegetables should be bright in color and tender-crisp.
Add chicken and stir sauce in. Serve over a bed of rice.

Meats

BARBECUED CHICKEN (For grill or stove top)

1/2 cup ketchup
1 Tbsp. lemon juice
1 tsp. chili powder
1/2 tsp. dry mustard
1 chicken, cut up

2 Tbsp. apple juice
1 Tbsp. soy sauce
1/2 tsp. salt
1/8 tsp. red pepper

Combine all ingredients except chicken in a large skillet or heavy pot. Add chicken pieces and turn to coat with sauce. Simmer covered 1 - 1 1/2 hours or until tender. Turn pieces at least once during cooking. If chicken starts to dry out, add some water.
If doing chicken on grill, brush with the sauce.

MARINADE FOR CHICKEN

1 cup milk or salad dressing
2 Tbsp. lemon juice
1 tsp. garlic powder
1/2 tsp. pepper

1/4 cup vinegar
1 Tbsp. oregano leaves
1/2 tsp. salt

Refrigerate chicken in marinade at least 20 minutes. Brush with marinade while grilling.

CHICKEN ALOHA

6 - 8 chicken breast halves or quarters
2 Tbsp. white grape juice concentrate, opt.
1 - 8 oz. can pineapple chunks with juice (or crushed is good too)
2 cups ketchup
1 green pepper, diced
1 Tbsp. mustard

Place chicken in large baking pan. Combine remaining ingredients and pour over chicken. Bake covered 375° F. for 1 hour. Uncover and bake an additional 15 minutes. Serve over a bed of rice.

Tips: Tough meat?
Pineapple, bananas, papaya, or kiwi are natural tenderizers. If you have tough meat, choose a recipe that has one of these fruits included, and add liquid to keep it moist. Do not allow to cook or bake dry;
(or)
Marinate in lemon juice 1 to 3 hours before cooking.

BAKED CHICKEN

Dip chicken pieces in:
beaten egg (or) mayonnaise

Roll in:
instant mashed potato flakes (or) whole grain flour

Place on greased pan and sprinkle with:
salt, pepper, paprika, or your favorite seasoning

Bake covered 325° F. for 1 hour. Uncover and bake 1/2 hour longer.

Hint: When deboning chicken, cut cooked chicken with scissors.

CHICKEN LOAF WITH PEAS

Mix in order given:

1 cup soft bread crumbs	2 cups milk or broth
2 eggs, beaten	1 tsp. salt
3 cups cooked diced chicken	1/4 tsp. paprika
1 cup cooked peas	

Pour into greased loaf pan. Bake at 350° F. for 1 hour. Let set 10 minutes before turning out of mold. Serve cold or hot with mushroom sauce.

MUSHROOM SAUCE

Saute in 1/4 cup melted butter:
1/4 pound fresh mushrooms or 1 - 6.5 oz. can mushrooms

Blend in:
6 Tbsp. flour

Continue stirring and add:
2 cups chicken broth

Cook until thickened.

Add:

1/4 cup milk or water	1 Tbsp. minced parsley
1 tsp. salt	1/2 tsp. lemon juice

CHICKEN LOAF WITH RICE

Mix in order given:
3 cups finely chopped chicken
2 cups fresh bread crumbs
2 cups cooked brown rice
2 Tbsp. chopped parsley or celery leaves
2 Tbsp. minced green pepper
1½ cups chicken broth
3 eggs, beaten
1½ cups milk or water
1½ tsp. salt
⅛ tsp. pepper

Shape into a loaf and bake 350° F. for 1 hour.
Serve with mushroom sauce *(See recipe on previous page)*.

> **Tip: Poultry spoils quickly.**
> Defrost in refrigerator 1 - 3 days; (or) place unwrapped meat in cold water or at room temperature 2 - 4 hours. Cook promptly. Refrigerate leftovers immediately.

BATTER OR BREADED FISH

(Batter and breaded fish often have sugar in them.)
Buy uncoated fish. After they are thawed squeeze water out.

Dip in:
beaten egg

Then roll in:
Mixture of whole grain flour and cornmeal with seasoning of your
choice: paprika, pepper, salt, lemon-herb blends, etc.

Fry in butter, or broil on greased pan on top shelf in oven at
450° F. for 10 - 20 minutes. Turn when just about done.

CODFISH PATTIES

1 cup codfish, cooked and flaked (do not overcook)
2 cups mashed potatoes $^1/_4$ tsp. salt
1 egg, beaten   1 small onion, minced
dash pepper

   Mix all ingredients. Heat 1 Tbsp. oil in heavy skillet. Drop by spoonfuls into skillet. Flatten slightly. Turn once. Can also be baked on greased cookie sheet 400° F. for 15 - 20 minutes. Put on broil last 5 minutes to brown.

CAJUN FISH

Preheat broiler 400° F.

In shallow pan, put:
$^1/_4$ cup buttermilk   2 tsp. mustard

In another pan, mix together:
$^1/_2$ cup cornmeal $^1/_8$ tsp. red pepper
1 tsp. salt $^1/_8$ tsp. black pepper
1 tsp. paprika   1 tsp. onion powder
$^1/_4$ tsp. garlic powder $^1/_2$ tsp. thyme

   Dip fish in buttermilk mixture, then in dry mixture. Place on greased cookie sheet. Put on top shelf and broil 10 - 15 minutes on each side.

LENTIL BURGERS

Combine in a bowl:
2 cups cooked lentils, cooled and drained
1 egg $\frac{1}{2}$ cup quick oats or bran
1 small onion   salt and pepper

Mix and add just enough ketchup to hold mixture together when made into patties. Fry like hamburgers in hot oil or butter, or bake 350° F. 10 minutes each side.   Serves 4

Beans, split peas, and lentils are high in fiber and protein. They can easily be used without meat in preparing a meal.

CARROT MEATLOAF

2 lbs. ground beef   3 eggs
$\frac{1}{2}$ cup milk or tomato juice   1 cup bread crumbs
2 Tbsp. prepared horseradish $\frac{1}{2}$ cup ketchup
2 carrots, finely shredded   1 medium onion, chopped
$\frac{1}{2}$ tsp. salt $\frac{1}{4}$ tsp. pepper

Mix all ingredients. Top with additional ketchup.
Bake 350° F. for 1 hour.   Serves 8 - 10

MEATLOAF

1 lb. ground beef   1 egg
$\frac{1}{2}$ cup tomato sauce or ketchup   1 small onion, minced
$\frac{1}{2}$ tsp. salt $\frac{1}{8}$ tsp. pepper
$\frac{1}{2}$ cup bread crumbs, wheat germ, or oat bran

Mix all ingredients. Put in loaf pan. Good with ketchup spread over top before baking.
Bake at 350° F. for 1 hour.   Serves 4 - 6

MEATLOAF SURPRISE

Your guests will enjoy this!

12 oz. shredded hash brown potatoes
1¹/₂ lb. ground beef
¹/₂ onion, minced
1 clove garlic, crushed
1¹/₂ tsp. salt
¹/₄ tsp. pepper

8 oz. pizza sauce
1 egg
1 tsp. paprika
¹/₂ cup rolled oats

Mix all ingredients together. Bake in 8 x 8" pan at 350° F. for 1 hour and 15 minutes. Pour off juice to make gravy.

Spread on meatloaf:

¹/₃ cup sour cream

¹/₂ cup shredded cheese

Return to oven 5 minutes or until cream is hot and cheese melts.

STUFFED PEPPERS

Cut in half:
3 large peppers

Remove seeds and pulp. Place in baking dish and fill with meat.

Must cut back on fats? For oven-baked hamburgers - put patties on greased baking sheet. Bake at 400° F. for 35 minutes.

Meat filling:
1 lb. ground beef
1 tsp. salt
¹/₄ cup ketchup or tomato juice

³/₄ cup brown rice, cooked
¹/₈ tsp. pepper
1 Tbsp. onion, minced

Top with additional ketchup.
Bake 350° F. for 1¹/₂ hours.

Note: Any meatloaf recipe may be used for filling.

PIZZA MEATLOAF

2 lb. ground beef
1 cup bread crumbs or oatmeal
1/2 cup grated Parmesan cheese
1 1/2 tsp. salt
1 cup pizza sauce

1/2 cup chopped onion
1/4 tsp. pepper
2 eggs
1 tsp. oregano

Mix and press into 8" square pan.
Bake 350° F. for 50 minutes. Pour off drippings. Spread ketchup over and 1 cup shredded mozzarella. Bake 15 minutes longer.

Time Saver: When browning ground beef, do as much as will fit in your skillet. Take out the extra and freeze it in pint boxes for quick casserole preparation later.

POOR MAN'S STEAK

3 lbs. ground beef
1 cup bread crumbs
1/4 tsp. pepper
1 - 6.5 oz. can mushrooms, chopped fine, undrained

2 tsp. salt
1 cup water

Mix all ingredients except mushrooms and pat into pan 1/2 - 3/4" thick.   May need two pans. Let set several hours or overnight. Cut into squares. Roll in flour and brown. Put meat in baking pan. Add 2 - 3 Tbsp. flour to the brownings in the pan. Blend mushrooms and a little water into brownings. Stir until bubbly and thickened. Add salt to taste.   Pour over meat. Bake 350° F. for 1 hour.   Serves 18 - 20

SALMON LOAF

2 - 14 3/4 oz. cans salmon
dash pepper
1 small onion, diced
1/4 cup ketchup

1/4 tsp. salt
1 egg
1/4 cup oatmeal

Mix all ingredients. Dump into loaf pan. Spread additional ketchup over top. Bake 350° F. for 1 hour.   Serves 6

TUNA PATTIES

1 egg, beaten
1 - 6 oz. can tuna, drained and flaked
$^1/_2$ cup rolled oats
$^1/_3$ cup shredded carrot
$^1/_4$ cup mayonnaise
2 Tbsp. onions, chopped
dash pepper

   Combine all ingredients, mixing well. Shape to form 3" patties. Brown in olive oil over medium high heat 3 - 4 minutes or until golden brown. Turn; continue cooking 3 - 4 minutes.

Opt. Melt slice of cheese on each patty last 2 minutes.

   Serve on bread or rice cake with tomato and lettuce if desired.

PICKLED TONGUE

   Cook beef tongue for 2 hours in water, with onion and 2 tsp. salt. After cooked remove skin. Save water for stock.

In kettle:
1 tongue, cut in bite size pieces
2 Tbsp. white grape juice conc.
4 Tbsp. vinegar

1 quart stock
dash pepper

   Cook 2 hours or more. Cool to serve. Keep in refrigerator in juice to store.
Note: A good meat to have in the summer when it's too hot to cook.

CABBAGE ROLLS

Prepare 1 pound ground beef as you would for meatloaf.
Cook 6 large cabbage leaves in water for 5 minutes.
Transfer to colander and refresh with cold water.
Divide meat in 6 parts and form in flattened balls.
Wrap cabbage leaves around balls, tucking edges under.
Place in baking pan.
Top with ketchup.
Bake 350° F. for 1 hour.

LIVER PATTIES

(A good way to get the children to eat their liver!)

Blend until smooth in blender:
1 lb. raw liver
1 egg
½ cup rolled oats
¼ tsp. salt
dash pepper
1 tsp. mustard

Add:
1 Tbsp. diced onion

Pour onto hot greased skillet in patties, like pancakes. Turn once.
Make a sandwich with bread, liver patty, mayonnaise, ketchup, mustard,
horseradish, cheese slice, etc.

Soups
and
Sandwiches

4 BEAN MEATLESS CHILI

Hint: Not only are beans high in fiber, but they are also high in protein. Give your system rest by having some meatless meals.

1/2 cup dried black turtle beans
1/2 cup dried navy, northern, pinto, or kidney beans
1/2 cup dried limas (or 1 pint frozen - add last half hour)
1 quart tomato juice *(See recipe for tomato juice cocktail)* **Delicious!**
1 cup blanched carrots, sliced or diced fine
1 clove garlic (remove garlic before serving)
1 small onion, minced
2 tsp. chili powder
1 pint green beans
1/2 tsp. salt
1 pinch oregano

Soak dried beans at least 8 hours. Discard soak water and cover with water again. Cook 1/2 hour. Add limas if using frozen and cook 1/2 hour more. Drain water off and add all ingredients. Heat and serve.

Serves 8 - 10

BROCCOLI CHEESE SOUP

4 cups chicken broth
2 cups chicken, cooked and cut up
2 tsp. chicken seasoning
1 large bunch broccoli, chopped and steamed
Opt: 1 cup shredded cheese or Velveeta
      2 cups shredded cooked potatoes

1 cup cold milk or water
1/2 tsp. salt
6 Tbsp. cornstarch

Hint: Make your own croutons! Toast bread in toaster or oven. Spread with butter and lightly sprinkle with garlic powder. Cut in small cubes.

Bring broth to a boil. Add seasonings and cornstarch to cup of cold milk. Stir into boiling broth. Cook for 2 minutes, stirring constantly. Add rest of ingredients. Heat and serve.
Sprinkle croutons over when eating.

Optional: Not fond of broccoli? Try adding noodles to the soup. Broccoli will be less noticeable.

Serves 8

CHICKEN BARLEY SOUP

Hint:
Add herbs to soup when nearly done to help retain their flavor.

1 quart chicken broth
³/₄ cup barley
1 Tbsp. chicken seasoning
1 bay leaf (remove after cooking)
¹/₂ tsp. pepper

1 pint diced cooked carrots
¹/₂ cup chopped onion
1 tsp. salt
¹/₂ tsp. poultry seasoning
¹/₂ tsp. dried sage

Simmer, covered, at least 1 hour. Remove bay leaf.

Opt. 1 - 2 cups cooked chicken may be added.

Serves 6

CHICKEN BROTH

Most canned broth you buy contains MSG and sugar. Make your own and freeze in pints or quarts.

In a large kettle place 4 lbs. chicken (whole or cut up). Cover with water and bring to a boil.

Add:

1 large onion, chopped
2 large carrots, diced

2 stalks celery, diced
1 garlic clove, opt.

Simmer 1¹/₂ - 2 hours. Cool ¹/₂ hour. Remove chicken, debone and place in small containers and freeze.

Freeze broth (skim fat off top before using).

CHILI SOUP

1 lb. ground beef
2 quarts tomato juice
2 tsp. chili powder
¹/₄ tsp. oregano

1 onion, chopped
¹/₂ tsp. salt
¹/₂ tsp. thyme
6 cups kidney beans
(or a mixture of beans)

Flooded with zucchini? Cut zucchini in bite size pieces and add to chili and vegetable soups.

Brown ground beef. Add chopped onion. Add seasonings to meat, then add remaining ingredients.

To thicken: Add a handful of quick oats and simmer several hours (or) stir in instant potato flakes just before serving.

60

VEGETABLE SOUP

Use chili recipe *(Previous page)*. Substitute a mixture of vegetables for 5 cups of the beans.

Can use: celery, carrots, peas, green beans, zucchini, lentils, etc.

HEARTY CHICKEN RICE SOUP

Combine:

1$1/2$ cups chicken broth
$1/2$ cup uncooked brown rice
$1/2$ cup carrots
1$1/2$ cups cooked diced chicken

3 cups cold water
$1/2$ cup celery
salt

Combine liquids, rice, and vegetables. Cover and simmer 25 minutes. Add remaining ingredients and continue simmering 35 minutes longer.

Opt. $3/4$ lb. Velveeta, added just before serving.   Serves 8

CREAM SOUP   (Substitute for Campbell's Soups)

6 Tbsp. butter
1 Tbsp. instant chicken seasoning
$1/4$ tsp. pepper

6 Tbsp. whole grain flour
$1/2$ tsp. salt
4 cups milk

In skillet mix all ingredients except milk. Heat until bubbly. Remove from heat and slowly blend in part of the milk. Return to medium heat and continue stirring in the rest of the milk as it thickens. Boil 1 minute, stirring constantly.

Store in refrigerator up to 1 week, or freeze in 1 - 2 cup containers up to 1 month.
Handy for quick casseroles.

Variations:
  Mushroom Soup - Add 4 oz. can finely chopped mushrooms.
  Celery Soup - Add 1 cup finely diced celery, cooked.
  Chicken Soup - Add $1/2$ cup finely chopped leftover chicken.

Note: Use rice milk if allergic to dairy products.

Using goat milk?
    When heating goat milk it tends to get that goaty taste.
Solution: When milking, cool milk fast. Milk directly onto a container of ice in the milk bucket. We use a quart freezer box. After milking, wash it and return it to the freezer for the next milking.
    Also, when heating milk, heat it as rapidly as possible. Turn the burner to medium-high or high, stirring constantly to keep from scorching. **Also:** Be sure the milk is fresh. Old milk gets a goaty taste.

HEARTY POTATO SOUP

1 lb. ground beef
3 Tbsp. flour
1 1/2 tsp. salt
4 cups cooked, shredded potatoes
dash pepper

1 onion, diced
4 cups milk
1/4 tsp. ginger
1/8 tsp. garlic powder
fresh parsley, chopped

Tip: A wonderful way to use leftovers:
Keep a bag or container in the freezer to accumulate leftover vegetables, noodles, rice, meat, etc. You can turn out delicious soups and casseroles with these!

Brown meat and onion. Stir flour into meat. Gradually stir in milk, stirring constantly until it boils. Add the rest of the ingredients and heat.   Serves 6 - 8

LENTIL SOUP

Brown:
1 lb. ground beef in soup kettle

Add:
6 cups broth or water
1/2 cup brown rice, uncooked
1 onion, diced

1 cup lentils, uncooked
1 cup carrots, diced

    Cook 3/4 hour.

Add:
1 Tbsp. chicken seasoning
1 tsp. salt

dash pepper
1 tsp. vinegar

    Simmer 15 more minutes.   Serves 8 - 10

SPLIT PEA SOUP

6 cups broth (or) 6 cups water + 1 Tbsp. instant chicken seasoning
1/2 tsp. salt
1 1/2 cup dried green split peas
2 stalks celery, diced
1 large carrot, diced
2 sprigs parsley, chopped

3/4 cup brown rice, uncooked
1 onion, diced
2 Tbsp. green pepper, diced
dash pepper
1 Tbsp. soy sauce

In kettle, mix ingredients except parsley and soy sauce. Simmer 1 hour. Add parsley and soy sauce. Simmer 5 -10 minutes. Serve with muffins, biscuits, or bread.   Serves 8 - 10

BBQ BEEF SANDWICHES

1 lb. ground beef
1 medium green pepper, chopped
1 Tbsp. date sugar or barley malt
1 Tbsp. vinegar
1/4 tsp. pepper
2 Tbsp. soy sauce

1/2 cup chopped onion
1 cup ketchup
2 Tbsp. mustard
1 tsp. salt
1 tsp. chili powder

Brown meat, onion, and pepper. Add rest of ingredients and simmer 1 hour.

Makes 6 - 7 sandwiches

PIZZA BURGERS   (For a crowd)

6 lb. ground beef (or part sausage)
2 Tbsp. whole grain flour
5 cups homemade pizza sauce
2 Tbsp. dried chopped onions
1-14 oz. jar Ragu pizza sauce
2 Tbsp. finely chopped pepper
3 thick slices Velveeta, opt.
2 cans mushrooms, chopped in blender

Fry ground beef. Stir in flour. Add sauce and stir until bubbly. Add rest of ingredients.

Toast buns 3 minutes. Put burger on and slice of cheese of your choice. Bake 350° F. for 3 - 5 minutes.

May be reheated or kept hot in crockpot until ready to serve.

Makes 50 pizza burgers

SLOPPY JOE

Brown:

4 lb. ground beef   1 cup chopped onion

Add:

1 pint homemade ketchup   5 Tbsp. mustard
13 oz. bought Sugarfree Ketchup   1 Tbsp. soy sauce
2 tsp. salt $1/4$ tsp. pepper
1 Tbsp. chili powder   1 cup rolled oats

Simmer 10 minutes.   Add more rolled oats if too thin.

Note: This recipe was designed to serve to guests.
If less sandwiches are desired, cut recipe in half or fourths.
All homemade ketchup can be used, but it won't taste as sweet.

Makes 24 sandwiches

Tip:
Leftover hamburger tomato gravy (for baked potatoes) can be turned into soup in the crockpot. Just add beans, juice, etc.

TUNA SANDWICH SPREAD

2 - 6 oz. cans tuna, drained   1 tomato, diced
1 stalk celery, diced   1 small pepper, diced
$1/8$ tsp. paprika $1/4$ cup mayonnaise

Mix and serve cold on bread or crackers.

Vegetables

ASPARAGUS CASSEROLE

2 cups asparagus
4 Tbsp. butter
4 Tbsp. flour (or 2 Tbsp. cornstarch)
2 cups milk

1 tsp. salt
1 cup grated cheese
6 hard boiled eggs, sliced

Hint:
    Use as little water as possible to cook vegetables. Start earlier and use lower heat. Retain those vitamins!

Cut asparagus in small pieces and cook in small amount of boiling salted water until just barely tender. Melt butter and blend in flour and salt. Add milk, stirring constantly until thickened. Add cheese and stir until melted. Layer half of asparagus, eggs, and cheese sauce in casserole. Repeat, ending with cheese sauce. Top with buttered bread crumbs. Bake at 350° F. until bubbly.

Serves 8

ASPARAGUS CHICKEN SUPREME

In greased 8 x 12" pan, spread:
4 cups blanched, cut asparagus, drained

Sauce:
1 Tbsp. butter
1 cup milk or broth
1 - 4 oz. can sliced mushrooms, undrained
1 cup shredded cheddar cheese
2 Tbsp. lemon juice
2 cups chicken, cut up

3 Tbsp. whole grain flour
1/2 cup mayonnaise

dash garlic powder

Pour sauce over asparagus. Cover with bread crumbs. Bake 350° F. for 40 - 45 minutes. Serve with rice or potatoes.

Note: Also good with broccoli instead of asparagus.

Serves 8 - 10

NOTE: Rice is more tasty if cooked in broth instead of water.

BUTTERNUT SQUASH

Peel, slice and dip in beaten egg.
Roll in a mixture of whole grain flour, salt, and pepper. Fry in butter.

BROCCOLI CHICKEN CASSEROLE

4 cups broccoli spears, steamed

3 cups chicken pieces

Sauce:

1/4 cup butter, melted

1/3 cup chicken broth

1/2 cup flour, stirred into 1/2 cup water

1/4 tsp. salt

1/4 tsp. pepper

2 cups milk or chicken broth

8 oz. shredded cheese or Velveeta slices

Spread broccoli and chicken in 13 x 9" pan. Set aside. In fry pan, melt butter. Stir flour in. Slowly blend chicken broth into flour. Add rest of ingredients, stirring constantly. Pour sauce over broccoli and chicken. Sprinkle buttered bread crumbs over top. Bake 350° F. for 1/2 hour or until bubbly.

Hint:
Vegetables stay fresh longer if they are not washed till just ready to use them.
Also try to gather them as close to cooking time as possible to retain nutritional value.

SCALLOPED CAULIFLOWER

1 head cauliflower

2 cups white sauce

1/4 tsp. pepper

1/4 cup grated cheese

3 hard boiled eggs

1/2 tsp. salt

1 cup buttered bread crumbs

Break cauliflower into pieces and cook in salt water till tender. Drain. Place alternate layers of cauliflower, sliced eggs, and white sauce in greased casserole.   Put crumbs and cheese on top. Bake uncovered 375° F. for 25 minutes.

Serves 6 - 8

Hint:
Yellow vegetables are rich in vitamin A. Green leafy vegetables are rich in A and B.

SPINACH LOAF

Mix together:

2 - 10 oz. packages frozen spinach, thawed and drained

4 eggs, beaten

2 Tbsp. whole grain flour

1 tsp. salt

Pour into greased 1 1/2 quart casserole.
Bake 350° F. for 45 minutes.
Opt: Melt Velveeta cheese over top just before serving.

Serves 6

DANDELION IN SWEET-SOUR SAUCE (Milk free)

Saute:
2 sugar free wieners, sliced
1½ Tbsp. butter or olive oil

Remove wieners from pan.

Add to butter:
2 rounded Tbsp. flour, stirring until browned.

Stir in gradually:

1 cup water
3 tsp. white grape juice concentrate

2 tsp. vinegar (or ReaLemon)
¼ tsp. salt (scant)

Cook about 5 minutes. Add wieners and simmer several minutes to blend flavors. Add a little more water if it gets too thick.

Add:
1 quart dandelion greens, cut up (approximately). Serve immediately.
May substitute spinach or other greens.   Serves 2 - 4

OVEN FRENCH FRIES

4 large baking potatoes, cut in long sticks - ³/₈" wide.

Put in large bowl of 1 quart ice water in refrigerator at least 15 minutes. Drain. Thoroughly pat dry with paper towels. Put potatoes in 1" layer in shallow pan. Drizzle ¼ cup olive oil over potatoes. With fork toss potatoes to coat evenly with oil. Preheat oven to 450° F. Bake 40 minutes, tossing potatoes every 10 minutes. Salt to serve.   Serves 4

HOMEMADE TATER TOTS

8 medium potatoes, cooked and peeled
4 rounded Tbsp. flour   1 tsp. salt
dash pepper   olive oil

Finely shred or use ricer while potatoes are hot. Stir in flour, salt, and pepper. Heat ¼" oil in heavy pan. Form into small balls and drop into oil. Fry until slightly golden. Drain on paper towels, then freeze for Tater Tot casserole, (or) to serve alone, bake in single layer on baking sheet at 400° F. until desired crispness.

Note:
The less vegetables are cooked, the more vitamins, minerals, and enzymes they retain. It is best to eat them raw or steamed.

ONION RINGS

Hint:
Refrigerating onions before slicing or chopping them reduces the tears. Store a few in the refrigerator.

Slice:
2 large onions in ³/₈" slices.   Separate into rings.

Put rings in large bowl of:
2 cups milk   2 cups ice water

Cover with plastic wrap.   Refrigerate 45 - 60 minutes. Drain and pat dry with paper towel.

METHOD # 1:
Dip rings in oil, then dip in mixture of:
1 cup whole grain flour
¹/₂ tsp. salt

METHOD # 2:
Batter:
1 cup whole grain flour   ¹/₂ tsp. salt
²/₃ cup water   1 Tbsp. butter
1¹/₂ tsp. baking powder   1 egg
¹/₂ tsp. lemon juice

Beat until smooth and dip rings in batter.
Place rings on greased cookie sheet.
Bake 350° F. for 20 - 30 minutes.

BAKED POTATO PANCAKES

1 lb. leftover baked potato pulp   ¹/₄ cup peppers, chopped
¹/₂ cup shredded cheddar cheese   1 small onion, chopped
1 egg, beaten   2 tsp. dried Italian herbs
salt and pepper to taste

Form into pancakes.   Coat with cornmeal.   Saute in oil until crisp and golden brown, turning once.

GOLDEN POTATOES

Toss together:
4 cups diced, boiled potatoes
1/4 cup chopped green pepper, opt.
1/4 lb. Velveeta cheese, cubed

1/4 cup chopped onion
1 slice bread, cubed
1 Tbsp. parsley

Put in greased casserole dish.

Heat together and pour over vegetables:
1/2 cup water
salt

3 Tbsp. butter
pepper

Bake uncovered 350° F. for 30 minutes, or until bubbly and browned.

PARTY MASHED POTATOES

9 large peeled potatoes, cooked
8 oz. cream cheese
1/4 tsp. pepper

1 tsp. salt
1 cup sour cream or yogurt
1/4 cup butter

In a large bowl, mash hot potatoes, then add softened cream cheese, sour cream, butter, and seasonings. Add milk if too thick. Pour in greased baking dish. Melt 1/4 cup butter and pour over potatoes. Next spread on 4 oz. cheddar cheese, and finally sprinkle with paprika. Bake uncovered 350° F. for 30 minutes. If refrigerated, bake 1 hour.

Serves 12 - 14

SCALLOPED POTATOES

6 medium potatoes, cooked and sliced thin
2 cups cream soup with mushrooms *(see page 61)*
1 small onion, chopped
1/8 tsp. pepper

1/2 tsp. salt
dash garlic powder

Mix together. Bake in covered casserole 350° F. for 1 hour.

Serves 8

Hint:
Potato skins are rich in minerals. Leave peels on whenever possible.

71

SCALLOPED POTATOES   (DAIRY FREE)

(This may sound strange, but it is delicious!)

Hint:
Add salt to vegetables after cooking. It takes less salt, and salt draws out the natural juices.

Simmer, covered, 20 minutes in skillet:

1/2 cup water   1 large sweet onion, sliced
1 clove garlic, or 1/8 tsp. garlic powder   black pepper, opt.
1 - 4 oz. can mushrooms, undrained   1/2 tsp. salt

Meanwhile thinly slice:
5-6 medium potatoes

Liquify ingredients in skillet in blender. Stir into potatoes. Pour back into skillet and simmer 1/2 - 1 hour or until tender.

Or place in casserole and bake covered 350° F. 50 - 60 minutes.

Serves 8 - 10

SPINACH MASHED POTATOES
(Your children will love this spinach!)

Peel, cook, and mash:
6 - 8 large potatoes

Add:
1 tsp. salt   1/4 cup butter
1/4 tsp. pepper   1 Tbsp. chopped chives
3/4 cup sour cream or yogurt   4 oz. cream cheese
1 - 10 oz. pkg. frozen spinach, chopped, cooked, and well drained
                                          (I blend it in the blender.)

Add milk if too stiff. Put in casserole.

Sprinkle with:
1 cup cheddar cheese

Bake 400° F. for 20 minutes.

Note: Can be made a day ahead and baked just before serving at 400° F. for 30 - 35 minutes. Can also be frozen.   Serves 8 - 10

TOMATO DUMPLINGS

In kettle, heat:

3 cups tomato juice   1/2 tsp. salt
1/8 tsp. pepper

Meanwhile, mix dumpling ingredients:

1 1/2 cups whole grain flour   1/2 tsp. salt
1 Tbsp. baking powder   1/2 cup apple juice

Drop dough from teaspoon (1 - 1 1/2" balls) into hot juice to form dumplings. Cover and cook 12 minutes. Do not remove cover while cooking. Serve at once.   Serves 4 - 6

ZUCCHINI CASSEROLE

Combine in large bowl:

8 cups diced unpeeled zucchini   1 cup bread crumbs
1 large green pepper, finely chopped   1/2 cup olive oil
1 large onion, finely chopped   salt and pepper to taste
2 large eggs, beaten   1 can mushrooms
2 Tbsp. fresh basil, chopped, (or) 2 tsp. dried
6 oz. shredded sharp cheddar cheese, opt.

Pour into 9 x 13" baking dish. Bake covered 350° F. for 45 minutes.
     Serves 8

ZUCCHINI PATTIES

2 cups grated zucchini   1 tsp. baking powder
1 cup cornmeal   1/4 cup Parmesan cheese
1/8 tsp. pepper   1/8 tsp. salt
2 eggs, beaten   1 Tbsp. mayonnaise

Mix and drop by spoonfuls in skillet in 2 - 3 Tbsp. hot butter. Fry until brown. May be served with tomato slice.

GERMAN POTATO SALAD

In a large skillet, saute in 2 Tbsp. butter or oil:
2 sugar free wieners, diced
$^1/_2$ onion, diced

Stir in:
2 Tbsp. whole grain flour
$^1/_4$ cup vinegar
1$^2/_3$ cups apple juice or white grape juice

Cook, stirring constantly, until bubbly and slightly thickened.

Add:
6 cups cooked potatoes, peeled and sliced

Stir gently.   Heat through.   Serves 8

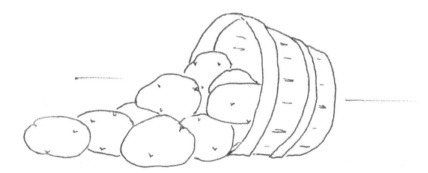

Salads

APPLE SALAD

Dressing:

1 egg	2 Tbsp. flour
1 cup apple juice	1 pinch salt

Blend together. Bring to a boil. Cook until thick. Blend in blender if lumpy.

Add:

a little vinegar to taste	lump of butter

Chill dressing.

4 - 5 diced apples - no need to peel (yellow and red are pretty)
3 sliced bananas
30 - 40 grapes, cut in half

Stir dressing into fruit.

Note: I make a double batch of dressing, and store the extra in the refrigerator for up to a week.

APPLE PINEAPPLE SALAD

1 can (20 oz.) crushed pineapple, undrained
2 Tbsp. barley malt or 1/4 tsp. stevia, opt.
1 pkg. (0.3 oz.) lemon flavored sugar-free jello
1 pkg. (8 oz.) cream cheese, softened
1 cup diced unpeeled apples
1/2 - 1 cup chopped nuts
1 cup chopped celery
1 Tbsp. frozen apple juice conc.
1 cup whipping cream, whipped until peaks form
1 1/2 tsp. vanilla
1 pinch salt

In a saucepan, combine pineapple and sweetener, and bring to a boil. Add jello; stir until dissolved. Remove from heat. Add cream cheese; stir until mixture is thoroughly combined. Cool. Fold in apples, nuts, and celery. Whip last 4 ingredients and fold into salad.

Note: Use sweet red apples for color.   Serves 9 - 12

FRUIT SALAD

Tip: When combining fruit and vegetable salads, strive for contrast in color, texture, form, and flavor. Appearance, as well as flavor, makes it appealing.

1 quart fruit cocktail
1½ cups crushed pineapple

    Drain juice from fruit to make dressing.

DRESSING:

Pour in blender:
drained juices plus pineapple juice to make 1 cup
½ tsp. lemon juice
1 - 1 oz. box sugar free lemon or vanilla pudding

    Blend on low speed until mixed. Chill.

Just before serving add:
3 - 4 bananas, sliced

FRESH FRUIT SALAD

Combine any fresh fruit of your choice: cherries, peaches, bananas, oranges, berries, etc. - approximate total of about 8 cups

    Add canned pineapple and other canned or frozen fruit if needed for more variety.

Cook together:
1 cup pineapple juice
2 Tbsp. cornstarch

    Stir constantly until thick. Cool. Stir in fruit.

Note: May stir orange or pineapple juice concentrate into fruit instead of thickened juice.

GIGGLE SALAD

1 cup carrots, grated
¼ cup raisins
1 cup crushed pineapple, drained
2 Tbsp. mayonnaise
¼ cup yogurt

    Mix all ingredients and refrigerate.

MOLDED APPLE SALAD (Served with cottage cheese)

Heat to boiling:
2 cups water

Soak:
1 - 0.3 oz. box sugar free strawberry banana jello
1 Tbsp. unsweetened strawberry or plain gelatin in:
drained pineapple juice with water added to make ½ cup

Add to boiling juice and stir until dissolved. Remove from heat.

Add:
½ cup frozen white grape juice concentrate
1 - 20 oz. can crushed pineapple, drained
1½ cups cold water
½ cup celery, finely diced
3 peeled, shredded apples
¼ cup walnuts, chopped

Pour into 6 quart ring mold. To serve, unmold onto plate and fill center with cottage cheese.

> **Tip: In a hurry to gel your salad?** Use part ice cubes for the cold water. Put cubes in cup and fill with water for each cup asked for.

CRANBERRY SALAD

In blender process:
4 cups orange juice
1 - 12 oz. bag fresh or frozen cranberries

Heat to boiling:
3 cups orange juice (to mold use ½ cup less juice)

Sprinkle over 1 cup cold orange juice:
1 - 0.6 oz. box strawberry sugar free jello
2 Tbsp. plain or flavored gelatin

Allow to soften 3 - 5 minutes. Stir into boiling juice. Remove from heat. Add cranberries.

When cool add:
2 - 3 stalks celery, chopped fine
10 large sweet apples, peeled and chopped

Serve with cottage cheese. The box of jello may be substituted with 2 Tbsp. plain gelatin.

> **Hint:** Try sweet apples like Yellow Delicious for extra sweetness in salads.

CARROT SALAD

Heat to boiling:
3 cups pineapple juice

Sprinkle:
4 Tbsp. orange gelatin over:
1 cup cold pineapple juice

Let set 3 - 4 minutes. Mix gelatin into boiling juice, stirring until dissolved. Remove from heat.

Add:
4 cups cold orange juice
4 cups crushed canned pineapple, undrained
2 Tbsp. lemon juice
$1/2$ tsp. salt

Add:
4 cups grated carrots when almost set

Note: For company, omit 2 Tbsp. gelatin and use 1 large box sugar free jello.

Note: To mold use 1 cup less liquid.

BROCCOLI AND CAULIFLOWER SALAD

(For special occasions, sugar free bacon is available at some grocery stores)

1 large head cauliflower, separated into bite size pieces
2 bunches broccoli, cut into florets
1 small onion, chopped fine
1 cup cheddar cheese, shredded
10 - 12 pieces bacon, fried and crumbled (or) Fakin Bacon bits

DRESSING:
$2 1/2$ cups mayonnaise
2 Tbsp. frozen white grape juice concentrate

Mix dressing and pour over everything except bacon or bacon bits. Refrigerate 2 - 24 hours, and add bacon when ready to serve.

Serves 20

LIME PEAR JELLO

Heat to boiling:
1¹/₂ cups pineapple juice

Allow to soak 3 - 4 minutes:
1 - 0.6 oz. box sugar free lime jello   ¹/₂ cup cold pineapple juice

Stir gelatin into boiling juice. Remove from heat.

Add:
2 cups juice drained from pears (or) white grape juice

Take 2 cups of the jello out and set aside.

Add:
2 - 8 oz. pkgs. cream cheese   1 Tbsp. lemon juice

Mix in blender.

Add:
2 cups diced pears

Chill. When slightly thickened, pour in 8 x 8" pan. Pour slightly thickened jello on top. Chill.

To mold:
Use ¹/₂ cup less juice. Put green jello in mold first, then cream cheese jello.

CRISP GARDEN SALAD

In saucepan:
1 Tbsp. plain gelatin   ¹/₄ tsp. salt
1¹/₄ cups pineapple juice

Stir over medium heat until gelatin is dissolved.   Remove from heat.

Add:
1 Tbsp. lemon juice   ¹/₈ cup vinegar (1 oz.)

Chill to unbeaten egg white consistency.

Stir in:
¹/₂ cup cucumber, diced   ¹/₂ cup celery, diced
¹/₂ cup carrots, finely shredded   2 tsp. onion, grated
2 Tbsp. green pepper, chopped

Turn into a 3 cup mold or in individual molds.   Chill until firm.

Unmold on salad greens.

Hint:
Perk up wilted lettuce by covering head of lettuce with cold water for 1 hour.   Drain.

Tomatoes for Thanksgiving? In the fall when it's time for frost and you still have green tomatoes in the garden, pick the healthy looking ones. Be careful to leave the stem on. Lay them on a layer of newspaper in a shallow cardboard box. Be sure none of them touch each other. Cover with one layer of newspaper. Check for ripe ones every 2 - 3 days.

CUCUMBER SLAW

4 cups sliced cucumbers $1/2$ cup onion, diced
1 cup green peppers, diced

DRESSING:
$3/4$ cup white vinegar $1/2$ tsp. celery seed
$1/4$ cup white grape juice concentrate $1/2$ tsp. salt

Stir all together.   Refrigerate.

LETTUCE SALAD

For a healthy salad:
Garnish lettuce salad with any of the following:

sliced hard boiled eggs	tomato
sliced radishes	sliced cucumbers
diced peppers	shredded raw red beet
scallions	chives
parsley	sprouts
sesame seeds	sunflower seeds
croutons	shredded carrots

Add dressing just before serving.

SEVEN LAYER SALAD

Put in 9 x 13" pan in order given:
1 head lettuce, torn in bite size pieces   1 cup frozen, uncooked peas
1 cup celery, diced   8 slices sugar free bacon
4 eggs, hard boiled and diced   (fried and chopped)

Mix and spread over top:
1 Tbsp. white grape juice conc.   2 cups mayonnaise

Top with:
4 oz. cheddar cheese, shredded

Cover and refrigerate 8 - 12 hours. When serving garnish with additional bacon.

Hint:
Iceberg lettuce has few vitamins. Mix it with romaine, green ice, bibb, or raw spinach; or eliminate iceberg lettuce altogether.

COLE SLAW

½-1 cup mayonnaise or Homemade Miracle Whip *(see recipe page 84)*
⅛ tsp. black pepper   ½ tsp. salt

Mix with:
1 medium head cabbage, shredded   1 Tbsp. onion, finely chopped
1 cup finely shredded carrot   ¼ cup celery, chopped

Chill at least 1 hour, or overnight. Stir again and serve.

Serves 8 - 10

Hint:
    When dry herbs are substituted for fresh, use only ⅓ the amount of dry herbs, as they are more concentrated.

GROW YOUR OWN SPROUTS

Measure 1 rounded Tbsp. sprouts into a wide mouth quart jar. Soak in lukewarm water for 8 hours. Drain and cover with purchased sprout jar cover or cheese cloth, and jar ring. Store upside down on back of your sink, with jar tilted a little to allow water to drain.

Rinse with room temperature water 3 times a day. (I make a habit of doing it when washing dishes at each meal.) They will keep longer if you rinse the hulls out. They are ready to eat in 3 - 4 days.   Refrigerate.

Buy your sprouting seeds at your food co-op or health food store to ensure that they are untreated.

Try alfalfa, mung bean, or clover. Radish or cabbage seeds are good in a mixture.

Tip: Healthy house-plants?
    When soaking seeds for sprouting, use the first water you pour off to water your plants.

POTATO SALAD

2 lb. boiled and peeled potatoes, diced or shredded
1 Tbsp. mild onion, chopped   6 eggs, diced
1 cup celery, finely diced   2 sprigs parsley, cut fine

Dressing:
1½ cups mayonnaise or Homemade Miracle Whip *(see recipe page 84)*
2 Tbsp. mustard   2 Tbsp. vinegar
2 Tbsp. apple juice concentrate   2 tsp. salt

Add a little water or milk if too thick.

CELERY SEED DRESSING

Tip:
If you have not yet acquired a taste for olive oil, use part olive and part of another variety. Use unrefined cold pressed oil.

In blender:

1 small onion (about 1 Tbsp.)   ¼ cup vinegar
1 tsp. dry mustard   ¼ tsp. salt

While blending above ingredients, very slowly add:
1 cup oil

Add:
1 Tbsp. celery seed
1½ cups mayonnaise or Homemade Miracle Whip. Blend until creamy.

FRENCH DRESSING

Can't have vinegar?
Try substituting lemon juice.

⅓ cup sugar free ketchup   1 tsp. salt
1 Tbsp. frozen apple juice concentrate   dash pepper
4 tsp. lemon juice   1 small onion
½ cup oil

   Blend all ingredients except oil in blender. Very slowly pour oil in while blending. Chill.

HOMEMADE MIRACLE WHIP

In blender, blend all together:
1 egg, plus apple juice to make ¾ cup
¾ cup oil   2 tsp. salt
½ tsp. dry mustard   1 Tbsp. lemon juice
dash paprika   ¼ tsp. garlic salt

In saucepan, heat to boiling:
1 cup apple juice   ⅓ cup white vinegar
¾ cup whole grain flour

   Add thick, hot mixture to blender mixture and blend until smooth. Cool.

VINEGAR AND OIL DRESSING

1 cup oil
2 Tbsp. lemon juice
1/8 tsp. black pepper

2 Tbsp. vinegar
1/4 tsp. salt
1/8 tsp. dry mustard

Combine all ingredients in a bottle or jar. Cover and store in refrigerator. Shake well to serve.

YOGURT DRESSING

1 cup yogurt
1 Tbsp. lemon juice
1 Tbsp. onion, chopped

1 Tbsp. oil
1 tsp. mustard
dash garlic powder

Blend all ingredients together.

THOUSAND ISLAND DRESSING

Stir together:
3/4 cup mayonnaise or Homemade Miracle Whip
1 Tbsp. chopped dill or sweet pickle
1 hard boiled egg, finely chopped
1 tsp. chili powder

1 tsp. onion, grated
1/2 cup ketchup
dash paprika

Fold in:
1 cup yogurt
Chill.

VEGETABLE DIP

Mix in blender:
2 cups mayonnaise
1/2 tsp. Mrs. Dash
dash garlic powder

1 - 8 oz. pkg. cream cheese
1/2 tsp. onion salt

Serve with raw vegetables.

BLENDER MAYONNAISE

In blender:
2 Tbsp. white vinegar
1 egg
1 Tbsp. lemon juice
$1/2$ tsp. salt
$1/2$ tsp. paprika
$1/2$ tsp. mustard
$1/4$ tsp. garlic powder
Mrs. Dash, opt.

Pour in very slowly while blending:
1 cup oil

Need just a squeeze of lemon? Prick a lemon deeply with a fork, and squeeze juice out. The lemon stays fresh longer than when it is cut.

"PHILLY" FRUIT DRESSING

Mix until well blended:
1 - 8 oz. pkg. Philadelphia cream cheese
$1/4$ cup orange juice
pinch of salt

Chill. Serve with fruit salad. Yummy with grapes, apples, and bananas.

FRUIT DIP

4 tsp. cornstarch
$1/2$ tsp. salt
1 cup unsweetened pineapple juice
2 Tbsp. lemon juice
2 eggs
8 oz. cream cheese
2 tsp. dry sugar free vanilla pudding mix, opt.

Combine cornstarch, salt, and juices in saucepan and cook, stirring constantly, until clear. Blend eggs in blender. Remove saucepan from heat and slowly pour eggs into mixture, stirring briskly. Cook over low heat, stirring constantly, for 3 - 5 minutes or until it begins to thicken. Pour into blender. Add cream cheese and pudding. Blend on low speed. Chill thoroughly. Serve with fresh fruit plate.

Cakes
and
Cupcakes

Tips for Whole Grain Baking

These recipes are all intended to use spelt flour; however, they are adaptable to whole wheat or any flour you desire.

Spelt flour is higher in protein than other grains, which is a real "plus" for anyone with sugar problems. It is highly nutritious and is easily digested.

Many people who are sensitive to wheat can tolerate spelts.

Spelt flour makes light yeast breads due to its high gluten content.

Try using T.V.P. (texturized vegetable protein) for a small part of the flour in your recipes to add more protein to counteract the sweets.

In cake and cookie recipes, substitute about 1/4 cup T.V.P. for 1/4 cup flour. In bread try using 1- 2 tablespoons to a batch of bread using 8 cups flour. Look for T.V.P. at your health food store or local Food Co-op.

Whole grain baked items are more dry and heavy, but tastier. Eat with fruit or milk.

If your family is hesitant to try these new foods, try using part white and part whole grain, gradually using less white and more whole grain flours.

Xanthan gum is a fiber similar to guar gum, and tends to improve the texture of baked goods. It is used as a binder, thickener, stabilizer, and emulsifier. Look for xanthan gum at your health food store. Use 1 teaspoon to 1 cup flour.

Sugar free baked items need to be refrigerated as they tend to spoil more quickly. Granola can be left at room temperature.

ANGEL FOOD CAKE

(This is not a real sweet cake. Wait to try it until your family has adjusted.)

Rinse a large mixing bowl with warm water and dry very thoroughly.

Beat until frothy:
1³/₄ cups egg whites (12 large), room temperature

Add:
¹/₂ tsp. salt
2 tsp. cream of tartar

Continue to beat just until whites are smooth, shiny, and stiff, but not dry.

Add:
1 tsp. almond extract
1 tsp. vanilla

Gradually beat in:
¹/₄ cup warmed white grape juice concentrate

Sprinkle by tablespoonfuls over whites, using a spatula to fold in just until mixed:
1 cup whole grain flour (room temperature)

Spoon batter into ungreased tube pan, rinsed with water.
Bake 325° F. for 1¹/₄ hours.
Invert pan until cool.

Tip for Mom's little helpers: Children can separate eggs. Have them break eggs open, one at a time, into a funnel placed over a cup. The white will pass through into the cup. Dump yolk out of funnel into another container.

MOCK ANGEL FOOD CAKE

Beat until stiff:

8 egg whites
2 tsp. cream of tartar

4 tsp. vanilla

Set aside.

In mixing bowl combine:

2²/₃ cups whole grain flour
2 Tbsp. baking powder
1 tsp. salt

¹/₂ cup barley malt or
1 tsp. stevia, opt.

Gradually pour over flour mixture, mixing with a spatula:
1¹/₃ cups warm apple juice concentrate

With spatula, carefully fold the egg whites in.
Bake in ungreased angel food pan at 350° F. for 45 minutes.

APPLE COBBLER

Place in 9 x 13" pan:

4 cups chopped apples or any fruit

1 tsp. cinnamon
¹/₄ tsp. nutmeg

Batter:

1 egg
2¹/₂ tsp. baking powder
1 Tbsp. barley malt or ¹/₄ tsp.
stevia, opt.
³/₄ cup milk or apple juice

2 cups whole grain flour
³/₄ tsp. salt
¹/₃ cup olive oil

Spiritual nugget:
Temptation becomes a sin when we yield to it.

Mix and pour over fruit.
Bake 400° F. for 25 minutes.

APPLESAUCE CAKE

Combine in large saucepan and cook until soft:
2 cups raisins
1¹/₂ cups water

   Cool, then drain.

Beat together:
1³/₄ cups applesauce
2 cups whole grain flour
¹/₂ tsp. nutmeg
¹/₄ cup barley malt or 1 tsp. stevia, opt.

2 eggs, beaten
1¹/₄ tsp. cinnamon
1 tsp. baking soda

   Add cooled raisins and mix. Pour into a greased 9 x 13" pan.
Bake 325° F. for 45 - 50 minutes.

<table>
<tr><td>**Hint:**
   Waxed paper can be used to line bottom of cake pans - no need to butter or oil pans. Saves calories and cleanup.</td></tr>
</table>

FAT FREE BANANA DATE CAKE

In mixer bowl beat:
4 eggs
1 tsp. vanilla

3 large bananas

Add:
2¹/₃ cups whole grain flour
¹/₂ tsp. cream of tartar
dash nutmeg

1¹/₂ tsp. baking soda
³/₄ tsp. cinnamon

In blender:
1 cup chopped dates
³/₄ tsp. soda

Pour into blender and process on high speed:
1 cup boiling water

   Add to batter and mix until just combined.
Pour into greased 8 x 12" pan.
Bake 350° F. for 30 - 35 minutes.

<table>
<tr><td>**Butter Substitute:**
   When converting your own recipes, applesauce or prune butter may be used 1:1 in place of butter. End product is sweeter and lower in fat.
   Hint: When making applesauce, save the pulp from the Victorio strainer. Run it through again. Use this thick sauce in place of butter.</td></tr>
</table>

CAROB CAKE WITH SOUR CHERRY TOPPING

Cream together:

3/4 cup olive oil

3 eggs

Add:

2 1/4 cups whole grain flour

1 tsp. baking soda

1 1/4 cups apple juice

7 Tbsp. carob powder

1 tsp. salt

Mix until just combined.
Pour into greased 8 x 12" pan.
Bake 350° F. for 40 minutes.

TOPPING:

Cook:

1 quart sour cherries

Add:

3 Tbsp. cornstarch dissolved in:
1/2 cup cold water

Cook 2 minutes longer, stirring constantly.

Add:

3 Tbsp. barley malt or 1 tsp. stevia

1/2 tsp. lemon juice

1 tsp. cinnamon

Cool.

After cake is baked, put:

8 oz. cream cheese on in slices and melt in oven 2 - 3 minutes, and spread over cake. Put cherry topping on last.

CAROB ZUCCHINI CAKE

Combine:
4 eggs
1 tsp. vanilla

1/2 cup olive oil
1/2 cup apple juice

Mix well.

Add:
2 1/2 cups whole grain flour
1 tsp. baking soda
1/2 tsp. cinnamon
1/4 tsp. salt
1/4 cup barley malt or 1 tsp. stevia

1/4 cup oat bran
1/4 cup carob powder
1/2 tsp. nutmeg
2 cups grated zucchini

Mix until just combined.
Pour into greased 9 x 13" pan.
Bake 350° F. for 60 - 65 minutes.

CARROT CAKE

Beat together:
4 eggs
3/4 cup crushed pineapple, drained

1/2 cup olive oil
1/2 cup applesauce

Add:
3 cups whole grain flour
2 tsp. baking powder
1/4 cup barley malt or 1 tsp. stevia, opt.

2 tsp. baking soda
2 tsp. cinnamon
1 tsp. salt

Stir in:
2 cups grated carrots

1 1/2 cups chopped nuts

Bake in greased 9 x 13" pan 350° F. for 1 hour.
Frost with any cream cheese frosting or icing. *(see page 105 or 106)*

DATE CAKE

Boil together:
1 cup chopped dates
1 tsp. baking soda

1½ cups apple juice

Add:
2 eggs, beaten

½ cup butter

Stir and then add:
1½ cups whole grain flour
½ tsp. salt

¾ tsp. baking soda

   Place in greased 8 x 12" pan.

Sprinkle over top:
½ cup chopped nuts
¼ cup date sugar, opt.

Bake 350° F. for 30 - 35 minutes.

DATE COFFEE CAKE

Beat together until creamy:
⅓ cup ripe banana, mashed
½ cup butter, softened

Beat in:
3 large eggs
1¼ cups apple juice

1 tsp. vanilla

Add and blend in:
2½ cups whole grain flour
1¼ tsp. baking soda

½ cup oat bran
2 tsp. baking powder

Stir in:
1½ cups chopped dates

   Spread in greased 9 x 13" pan.

Combine and sprinkle over batter:
⅓ cup chopped dates
⅓ cup chopped nuts
⅓ cup coconut

   Bake 350° F. for 25 minutes. Cool.

100%
Whole
Grain

GINGERBREAD

Beat until foamy:
1/2 cup molasses
1 tsp. baking soda

Add and beat:
1/2 cup butter, melted
3 eggs

Add:
3 cups whole grain flour
1 tsp. ginger
1 tsp. cinnamon
1 tsp. vanilla
1/4 cup barley malt or 1 tsp. stevia, opt.

Dissolve:
1 tsp. baking soda in:
1 cup buttermilk or apple juice

Add to rest of ingredients. Mix until smooth.
Bake in greased 8 x 12" pan at 350° F. for 45 minutes.
Serve with raisin sauce or milk.

RAISIN SAUCE:

Blend together in saucepan:
2 Tbsp. butter, melted
2 Tbsp. whole grain flour

Remove from heat and slowly blend in:
2 cups apple cider
1/2 cup raisins

Bring to a boil, stirring constantly. Cook 1 minute. Remove from heat. Serve hot over gingerbread.

Hint:
Whole grain flour varies. You may need only 7/8 cup per cup of white flour.
If you are making your own, you may discover that flour has more moisture soon after the grain is harvested, at which point you will likely need the full amount of whole grain flour.

GRANDMA'S FRUITCAKE

Cook 3 minutes:

2 cups dried fruit mixture   1 cup raisins
1 cup cider

Add:

2 tsp. baking soda   1 Tbsp. butter
1 cup peanut butter   1/2 tsp. maple flavor
1/3 cup barley malt or 1 tsp. stevia, opt.

Blend until fine and add to fruit mixture:

4 eggs   1 1/2 cups prunes
4 1/4 Tbsp. water

Add:

2 cups whole grain flour   1/2 tsp. salt
1 tsp. cinnamon   1 cup chopped nuts

Put in greased angel food pan.
Bake 325° F. for 1 1/2 hours.

Dried fruit mixture is available in health food stores, or make your own, using dry apples, bananas, pineapple, and papaya. Add raisins and dates.

HOLIDAY FRUITCAKE

Boil 3 minutes, stirring constantly:

4 cups dried fruit mixture   3 cups raisins
1 cup dates   2 cups grape juice conc.

Remove from heat and add:

1 cup butter   1/2 tsp. baking soda

In mixer bowl, beat:

4 eggs, beaten   1 1/2 tsp. cinnamon
3 cups whole grain flour   1/2 tsp. nutmeg
1 1/2 tsp. baking powder   1/2 tsp. allspice
1 tsp. salt   1 cup chopped walnuts

Add fruit mixture. Fill 2 greased loaf pans or one angel food pan.
Bake 300° F. for 2 1/2 hours.
Refrigerate before cutting.

Tip:
Fruitcake is best if refrigerated 1 - 2 days before eating.

PEACH CAKE

Beat together:

4 eggs
1½ cups pineapple juice (or apple)
½ cup olive oil
4 tsp. vanilla

Add and mix until just combined:

4 cups whole grain flour
1 tsp. cream of tartar
½ cup barley malt or 1½ tsp.
            stevia, opt.
3 tsp. baking soda
½ tsp. salt
6 cups peaches, diced

   Pour batter into greased 9 x 13" pan.
Bake 350° F. for 1 hour.
Serve topped with sliced peaches or whipped cream.

PEACH UPSIDE-DOWN CAKE

8 cups fresh or canned peaches, chunked
2 tsp. cinnamon

Topping;

½ cup butter
2 eggs
½ cup applesauce or prune butter
1½ cups apple juice or milk
2 tsp. vanilla
1 cup whole grain flour
4 tsp. baking powder
3 Tbsp. barley malt or
     1 tsp. stevia, opt.

   Place peaches in 9 x 13" pan. Sprinkle cinnamon over peaches.
Mix topping together and pour over peaches.
Bake 350° F. for 40 - 45 minutes.

Note: Also good with berries in place of peaches.

PINEAPPLE CAKE

Beat:

¹/₂ cup butter, melted
2 eggs

1 tsp. vanilla

Add:

1 - 20 oz. can juice packed pineapple chunks, undrained
¹/₂ cup unsweetened orange juice ¹/₂ cup raisins
2 cups whole grain flour 1 tsp. baking soda
1 tsp. baking powder

Pour into 9 x 13" greased pan.
Bake 325° F. for 45 minutes. Immediately cover with foil after removing from oven.   Cool.

Optional crumb topping:

1 Tbsp. butter, softened 1 Tbsp. whole grain flour
2 Tbsp. date sugar 2 Tbsp. oat bran

Bake cake 25 minutes at 325° F.
Put topping on and bake 20 minutes longer.

PUMPKIN CAKE

In large bowl beat:

4 eggs

Add and continue beating:

1 cup olive oil 16 oz. pumpkin
1 tsp. vanilla

Add and mix on low speed until just mixed:

2 cups whole grain flour 2 tsp. baking soda
¹/₄ tsp. cream of tartar ¹/₂ tsp. salt
1 Tbsp. cinnamon ³/₄ tsp. ground cloves
³/₄ tsp. ginger ¹/₂ tsp. nutmeg
¹/₂ cup barley malt or 2 tsp. stevia, opt. ¹/₂ cup chopped pecans or
walnuts

Do not over beat. Pour into greased 8 x 12" pan.
Bake 350° F. for 60 minutes.

Note: Delicious served with applesauce, or Cream Cheese Frosting.

RHUBARB CAKE

2 eggs, beaten
1/2 cup butter, softened
1/4 cup barley malt or 1 1/2 tsp. stevia, opt.
2 tsp. baking soda dissolved in:
     2 cups apple juice

1/2 cup applesauce
2 tsp. vanilla
4 cups whole grain flour
2 tsp. salt
3 cups diced rhubarb

Mix and pour into a greased 9 x 13" pan.

Sprinkle over batter:
1 tsp. cinnamon

Bake 350° F. for 60 minutes.

RHUBARB COFFEE CAKE

Beat together:
1/2 cup applesauce
1/4 cup barley malt or 2 tsp. stevia, opt.

1 egg
1 tsp. vanilla

Add:
2 cups whole grain flour
1 tsp. baking soda

1/2 tsp. salt
1 cup apple juice

Fold in:
1 1/2 cups chopped rhubarb

Pour into greased 8 x 12" pan.

Sprinkle over batter:
1/2 cups chopped nuts

1 tsp. cinnamon

Bake 325° F. for 50 minutes.

> **Hint:**
> Raw diced rhubarb can be frozen to be used for winter cakes, pies, etc.
> It supplies vitamin A and B, as well as calcium and iron.

Tip: Prune butter for fat free baking:

Tip: Prune butter for fat free baking:
Substitute 1 to 1 for butter, margarine, or oil. Combine in blender and puree: 1 1/3 cups (8 oz.) prunes and 6 Tbsp. water.
(or) You can also cook them until very soft and thickened, and mash them.
(or) You can substitute a jar of baby food prunes using the 1 to 1 ratio.

RHUBARB STRAWBERRY UPSIDE-DOWN CAKE

Layer in 8 x 12" baking dish:
3 - 4 cups rhubarb, diced
2 cups strawberries, fresh or frozen
1/4 cup apple juice if using frozen berries, 1/2 cup if using fresh

Topping:
1/4 cup prune butter or applesauce
2 Tbsp. barley malt or 3/4 tsp. stevia, opt.
1/2 cup whole grain flour
1 tsp. vanilla

1/4 cup butter, softened
1 egg
2 tsp. baking powder
3/4 cup milk or apple juice

Beat until just combined.
Spread over fruit.
Bake 350° F. for 40 minutes.

STRAWBERRY SPONGE SHORTCAKE

3 egg whites
pinch of salt
3 egg yolks
3 Tbsp. barley malt or 1 tsp. stevia, opt.

1 cup whole grain flour
1 tsp. baking powder
5 Tbsp. apple juice conc.

Beat egg whites and salt until stiff, but not dry. Set aside.
Beat remaining ingredients together and fold into egg white mixture.
Bake in 9" square pan at 350° F. for 20 minutes.
Serve with strawberries and whipped cream.

OATMEAL CAKE

Combine and let set 20 minutes:
2¹/₂ cups boiling apple juice
2 cups rolled oats

<table>
<tr><td>

Hint:
    When baking cakes, place batter higher in the corners and edges of the pan than in the center.

</td></tr>
</table>

Beat together:
1 cup butter   4 eggs
2 tsp. vanilla

Add:
oatmeal mixture   2²/₃ cups whole grain flour
¹/₄ cup barley malt or 2 tsp. stevia, opt.   2 tsp. baking soda
1 tsp. salt   1 tsp. baking powder
2 tsp. cinnamon

Bake in a greased 9 x 13" pan at 350° F. for 45 - 50 minutes.

TOPPING:

¹/₂ cup butter, melted   1 cup coconut, unsweetened
1 cup chopped nuts   1 tsp. vanilla
¹/₄ cup white grape juice concentrate

  Spread over baked cake.
Broil several minutes until browned. Watch carefully!

TEXAS SHEET CAKE

Hint: Buttermilk and sour milk can be used interchangeably.

If you don't have any of either, make 1 cup sour milk by placing 1 Tbsp. lemon juice into cup and fill with milk. Let set 5 minutes.

Bring to a boil in saucepan:
1/2 cup butter
1 cup apple juice

4 Tbsp. carob powder

Dissolve:
1 1/2 tsp. baking soda in:
1/2 cup buttermilk, yogurt, or apple juice

Add to hot mixture (be sure your kettle is large enough or it will foam up and run over).

In mixer bowl, combine:
2 eggs
1/4 cup barley malt or 1 tsp. stevia, opt.

1 tsp. vanilla
1/2 tsp. salt

Add hot mixture alternately with:
2 cups whole grain flour

Batter will be thin.
Bake in greased jelly roll pan 350° F. for 20 minutes.

Note: (For egg allergies) This cake is good with 2 bananas in place of eggs.

BANANA CUPCAKES

Beat:
1/2 cup olive oil
2 eggs

3 ripe bananas

Add:
2 cups whole grain flour
2 Tbsp. barley malt or 1/2 tsp. stevia, opt.
3/4 tsp. salt

1 tsp. baking soda
1/2 tsp. baking powder
1/4 cup apple juice conc.

Beat until just mixed. Fill paper cake cups 2/3 full.
Bake 350° F. for 20 minutes.

CAROB CUPCAKES

Beat:
1/2 cup butter, melted
1/2 cup carob powder

2 eggs

Add:
1/2 cup barley malt or 2 tsp. stevia, opt.
1 tsp. baking powder
1/2 tsp. salt
1 cup apple juice

1 3/4 cups whole grain flour
1 tsp. baking soda
1 tsp. vanilla
1 1/4 cups rolled oats

Fill paper cake cups 2/3 full.
Bake 350° F. for 25 minutes.

Frost and decorate with nuts.

Yield: 1 1/2 dozen cupcakes

DATE CUPCAKES

Pour:
1/2 cup boiling apple juice over:
1 cup dates
3/4 tsp. baking soda

Add:
1/4 cup butter

Set aside.

Beat:
1 egg
1 1/2 tsp. vanilla

1/2 cup ripe banana

Add:
1 1/2 cups whole grain flour
1/4 tsp. salt

1 1/4 tsp. baking powder

Add:
date mixture

1/4 cup chopped nuts

Fill paper cake cups 2/3 full.
Bake 350° F. for 20 minutes.

Yield: 1 dozen cupcakes

ZUCCHINI CUPCAKES

Hint: When something special is coming up such as a holiday banquet where all sorts of goodies will be served, **be sure to have some special sugar free treats at home**. This will make it easier to say "no".

If you have a carry-in, take along a delicious sugar free dessert.

Mix:
3 eggs, beaten
1/4 cup barley malt or 1 tsp. stevia, opt.
2 cups whole grain flour
1/2 tsp. baking powder
1/2 tsp. salt

1 cup olive oil
2 tsp. vanilla
1 cup oatmeal
2 tsp. baking soda

Add:
2 cups grated zucchini
1 cup coconut

1 cup chopped nuts

Fill paper cake cups 2/3 full.
Bake 350° F. for 25 minutes.

Yield: 2 dozen cupcakes

BOILED FLOUR ICING

(For whoopie pies or anything)

In saucepan:
5 Tbsp. flour
1 cup apple juice

Cook, stirring constantly, until thickened. Mixture will be very thick. Cool thoroughly.

Beat together:
1 cup butter
1/2 tsp. vanilla

Add flour mixture and beat until very fluffy, 5 or more minutes.
Variation: Add 2 1/2 Tbsp. carob powder to flour mixture.

CAKE DECORATING ICING

1/2 pint cream
pinch salt
1 Tbsp. white grape juice conc.
1/2 tsp. vanilla
2 - 8 oz. pkgs. Philadelphia cream cheese, room temperature
2 Tbsp. powdered milk, approximately

Whip first 4 ingredients in a chilled bowl until soft peaks form. Add cream cheese and mix. While whipping at medium speed, add powdered milk until desired consistency.

Note: For a sweeter icing for special occasions, use sugar free vanilla pudding (dry) in place of powdered milk.

Note: Take your birthday pictures the same day you decorate, as this icing tends to dry out and crack.

> **Spiritual nugget:**
> Take a few minutes to pause beside the still waters of God's Word. Drink deeply and you will find it cool and refreshing.

CAROB FROSTING

Combine in saucepan:
1 Tbsp. butter
1/2 cup apple juice
1/2 cup carob powder
1 tsp. vanilla

Heat over low heat, stirring constantly until smooth. Pour onto cake or brownies. Spread out and chill.

CAROB BANANA ICING

2 cups mashed ripe bananas
1 tsp. vanilla
1 3/4 cups carob powder
2 Tbsp. whole grain flour

Beat all ingredients on high speed for 2 - 3 minutes. Spread on warm cake. Makes enough frosting for a sheet cake.

CAROB PEANUT BUTTER FROSTING

½ cup carob powder   1 cup apple juice

    Cook 3 - 5 minutes, stirring constantly until smooth.

Add:

7 Tbsp. peanut butter   6 Tbsp. apple juice conc.
1 tsp. vanilla
Stir until smooth.
Spread over brownies or cake while warm.
Chill.

Tip: Did you know that some brands of vanilla contain sugar?

CAROB ICING

2 Tbsp. cornstarch   1½ Tbsp. carob powder
1 cup apple juice   ½ tsp. vanilla

    In a saucepan, stir the cornstarch and carob powder together.
Stir in the apple juice.
Bring to a boil, stirring constantly. Boil 3 minutes.
Remove from heat and add vanilla.
Spread over brownies or cake while still warm.
Chill.

FROSTING

1 - 8 oz. pkg. cream cheese, softened
¼ cup yogurt
1 tsp. vanilla

    Beat cream cheese in small bowl until smooth. Add yogurt and vanilla. Beat until smooth and thick.

Add <u>one</u> of the following:

    ¼ cup coconut
    3 Tbsp. carob powder
    ⅓ cup fruit, chopped fine (strawberries, cherries, blueberries,
                blackberries, crushed pineapple, etc.)

Cookies,
Brownies
and Bars

See page 88 for tips on whole grain baking.

APPLE BUTTER BARS

Mix together:
1/2 cup butter, melted
1/2 cup nuts, chopped

1 cup whole grain flour

   Press mixture into an 8 x 12" pan.
Bake 350° F. for 10 minutes.

Spread on:
2 cups apple butter or pear butter

Mix together:
1/2 cup butter, melted
1/4 tsp. baking soda
1/2 cup rolled oats

1 cup whole grain flour
1/2 tsp. salt
1/4 cup oat bran

   Sprinkle over bars.
Press gently into apple butter.
Bake 350° F. for 25 - 30 minutes.

> **Hint:**
>   Sugar free baked goods need to be stored in the refrigerator as they tend to spoil more quickly.
>   Granola and crackers can be left at room temperature.

APPLE BARS

CRUST:

Combine:
2 1/2 cups whole grain flour
1 tsp. salt
1 cup butter
1 egg yolk and enough milk or juice to make 2/3 cup

   Put half of crust in jelly roll pan.

Top with:
2 handfuls sugar free corn flakes
8 - 10 apples, grated
1 - 2 tsp. cinnamon

   Put top crust on.

Beat and put on top:
1 egg white

   Bake at 350° F. for about 40 minutes.

Note: Tastes best when freshly made.

100 %
Whole
Grain

FRESH APPLE BARS

Why olive oil?
Olive oil can withstand higher heat without becoming carcinogenic (cancer causing).

It is excellent for people watching their cholesterol.

Beat well:
6 eggs
2 cups olive oil (or) 1 cup oil and 1 cup applesauce

Add:
4 cups whole grain flour
2 tsp. baking soda
1/2 tsp. cream of tartar
1 tsp. salt
1 tsp. cinnamon
1/2 cup barley malt or 2 tsp. stevia, opt.

Fold in:
4 cups apples, pared and sliced

Pour batter into greased jelly roll pan.
Bake 350° F. for 40 - 50 minutes.

GOLDEN APPLE BARS

1/2 cup butter, softened
1/4 cup barley malt or 1 tsp. stevia, opt.
1 tsp. vanilla
2 tsp. baking powder
1 cup chopped raw apples

1/4 cup applesauce
2 eggs, beaten
2 cups whole grain flour
1/4 tsp. salt

Mix together and spread in greased 9 x 13" pan.
Bake 350° F. for 30 minutes.   Cool and cut in bars.

APPLESAUCE CAROB BROWNIES

1 cup butter, melted
4 eggs
4 Tbsp. apple juice concentrate
1 cup applesauce
2 tsp. vanilla
1 cup carob powder

2 cups whole grain flour
1/2 cup oat bran
1 tsp. baking powder
1 tsp. baking soda
1 cup nuts, chopped

Combine all ingredients in order given. Spread on greased jelly roll pan.
Bake 350° F. for 25 minutes. Spread Carob Frosting on *(page 105)*.
Chill.

CAROB DATE BROWNIES
Beat:
6 Tbsp. butter, melted
6 eggs

1 1/3 cups applesauce
4 tsp. vanilla

Add:
1 cup chopped dates
1/2 cup oat bran
2 tsp. baking powder

2 cups whole grain flour
1 cup carob powder

Mix well. Spread in greased jelly roll pan.
Bake 375° F. for 25 minutes.
If desired, frost with Carob Frosting *(page 105)*.
Cool.

> **Hint:**
> **Have a craving for chocolate?**
> Try taking a magnesium supplement for a while - it is believed that it is actually the magnesium in the chocolate that some people crave.

CHEWY BROWNIES

2/3 cup olive oil
4 eggs
1 cup banana, mashed
1/2 tsp. vanilla
1/2 cup white grape juice concentrate

2 cups whole grain flour
2/3 cup carob powder
1/2 tsp. baking soda
1/2 tsp. cream of tartar
1 1/3 cups rolled oats

Combine wet ingredients and beat well. Add flour and carob powder.   Beat again. Add rest of ingredients, beating until just mixed.
Bake 350° F. for 30 - 35 minutes.

BLACK BOTTOM BANANA BARS

(You'll love these!)

Beat:

$^1\!/_2$ cup butter, melted $^1\!/_2$ cup applesauce
2 eggs   2 tsp. vanilla
3 cups mashed ripe bananas (about 6 medium)
2 Tbsp. barley malt or $^1\!/_2$ tsp. stevia, opt.

Add:

$2^1\!/_2$ cups whole grain flour $^1\!/_2$ cup oat bran
2 tsp. baking powder   2 tsp. baking soda
1 tsp. salt

   Mix all together. Divide batter in half.

Add:

$^1\!/_2$ cup carob to half of batter.

   Spread in greased jelly roll pan. Spoon remaining batter on top and spread over all.
Bake 350° F. for 25 minutes.

Note: Allergic to eggs? Omit the eggs and add 2 extra bananas. Blend all bananas until smooth.

Delicious and good texture!

BANANA SOUR CREAM BARS

Beat:

$^1\!/_2$ cup butter, softened   2 eggs
1 cup sour cream or yogurt   2 tsp. vanilla
2 cups mashed bananas (about 4)

Add:

$^1\!/_4$ cup barley malt or 1 tsp. stevia, opt.   2 cups whole grain flour
$^1\!/_2$ cup oat bran   1 tsp. salt
$1^1\!/_4$ tsp. baking soda $^1\!/_2$ cup chopped nuts

   Mix and spread on greased jelly roll pan.
Bake 375° F. for 25 minutes.

BLUEBERRY BARS

Crust:

¼ cup butter, softened   1 cup whole grain flour
¼ cup applesauce

  Mix and spread in greased 8 x 8" pan.
Bake 350° F. for 25 minutes.

Mix together:

2 eggs, beaten	½ tsp. baking powder
¼ cup barley malt or 1 tsp. stevia, opt.	¼ tsp. salt
½ tsp. cinnamon	1 tsp. vanilla
1 tsp. lemon juice	½ cup coconut
¼ cup whole grain flour	¾ cup chopped walnuts
1½ cups blueberries, fresh or frozen	

  Spread over top of baked cookie base. Sprinkle more nuts over top if desired.
Bake 30 minutes. Cool. Cut into bars.

> **Prune butter for fat free baking:**
>
>   Combine in blender and puree:
> 1⅓ cups (8 oz.) pitted prunes with 6 Tbsp. water. Substitute prune butter 1 to 1 for butter, oil, or margarine called for in recipe.
>
>   You can also cook them until very soft and thickened, and mash them (or you can use pureed baby food prunes with 1 to 1 ratio.

CRISPY CAROB BARS

Delicious!

½ cup butter, melted	¼ cup olive oil (or) prune
3 eggs, beaten	1 tsp. vanilla butter
3 Tbsp. barley malt or 1 tsp. stevia, opt.	1⅓ cups whole grain flour
½ tsp. baking powder	½ tsp. salt
3 Tbsp. carob powder	½ cup chopped nuts

  Mix and spread in greased jelly roll pan.
Bake 350° F. for 15 - 18 minutes.

Remove from oven and spread:

8 oz. cream cheese over cake
 (I put slices on, and warm in oven a few minutes, and then spread it out.) Cool.

Topping: Cook over low heat, stirring constantly until well blended:
1½ cups malt sweetened carob chips   1¼ cups peanut butter
3½ Tbsp. butter

  Remove from heat.

Stir in:

2 cups crisp brown rice cereal

  Spread over bars immediately. Chill.

CAROB CHIP BARS

²/₃ cup butter

3 eggs

1 tsp. vanilla

³/₄ cup barley malt or 2 tsp. stevia, opt.

¹/₂ cup chopped nuts

2 cups whole grain flour

1 tsp. baking soda

¹/₂ tsp. cream of tartar

¹/₂ tsp. salt

³/₄ cup carob chips

Beat liquid ingredients together. Add dry ingredients. Mix until just combined. Fold in nuts and carob chips.
Bake in greased 9 x 13" pan at 350° F. for 30 minutes.

DATE PINWHEELS

Beat:

1 cup butter, melted

3 eggs

Add:

4 cups whole grain flour

¹/₄ cup barley malt or ³/₄ tsp. stevia, opt.

¹/₄ tsp. salt

1 tsp. vanilla

1 tsp. baking soda

Mix and add extra flour if needed to make a stiff dough. Divide into 3 parts. Roll out on saran. Spread with date filling. Roll up like a jelly roll. Roll in saran and refrigerate. Cut in ¹/₄" slices.
Bake 375° F. for 10 - 15 minutes.

Filling:

1¹/₂ lbs. dates

1 cup chopped walnuts

1¹/₈ cups apple juice

Cook dates and juice until thick.   Add nuts and cool.

Spiritual nugget:
Salvation is free, but discipleship is costly.

DATE SQUARES

Date filling:
2 cups chopped dates   1¹/₃ cups fruit juice or water

Cook until smooth. Cool.

Crumbs:
³/₄ cup butter   2 cups whole grain flour
2 cups oatmeal   pinch salt
1 tsp. baking soda   ¹/₄ cup fruit juice

Mix and put half of crumbs in greased 8 x 12" pan. Spread date filling on. Put rest of crumbs evenly over top.
Bake 350° F. for 45 minutes.

FRUIT BARS

1 cup dates   2 cups whole grain flour
1 cup raisins   2 tsp. baking soda
1 cup apples, peeled and chopped   ¹/₂ tsp. salt
2 cups apple juice   4 eggs
1 cup butter   2 tsp. vanilla
1 cup chopped walnuts

Boil fruit and juice.   Add butter.   Mix eggs, vanilla, and dry ingredients.   Add fruit mixture.
Bake in greased jelly roll pan at 350° F. for 25 - 30 minutes.
Cool slightly and cut in bars.

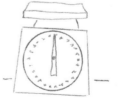

MOIST FRUIT BARS

Boil for 3 minutes:

1 cup raisins

1/2 cup crushed pineapple

1/2 cup chopped dates

1 cup water

Add:

1/2 cup butter

In mixer bowl:

2 eggs, beaten

1 cup whole grain flour

1 tsp. baking soda

1 tsp. vanilla

1/4 cup oat bran

1 cup chopped nuts

Mix. Add fruit mixture and mix again.
Place in a greased 8 x 12" pan.
Bake 375° F. for 25 minutes.

GRANOLA BARS

Hint: Keep wheat germ refrigerated to preserve the vitamins.

In saucepan, combine and bring to a boil:

1 1/2 cups cider or apple juice

1 cup chopped dates

1 cup raisins

Add:

1/4 cup butter

Mix:

1 egg

1 tsp. vanilla

1/4 cup wheat germ

1 cup chopped nuts

4 cups rolled oats

1 tsp. cinnamon

Add:

cooked mixture

Spread in a greased 8 x 12" pan. Dip hands in water to smooth out batter.
Bake at 350° F. for 35 - 40 minutes. Cool and then cut.

HAWAIIAN BARS

Tip:
    Bake cookies on the top rack of the oven.

Filling:
1 - 20 oz. can unsweetened crushed pineapple with juice
2 cups chopped dates   1 Tbsp. vanilla

Dough:
1 cup whole grain flour   1/2 cup coconut
1/2 cup chopped walnuts   3 cups rolled oats
1/2 cup applesauce   1/2 cup orange juice
1/4 cup olive oil or butter

   Cook filling until thick. Set aside. Mix dough together. Spread half of dough in a greased 8 x12" pan. Spread filling over. Cover with rest of the dough.
Bake 350° F. for 35 minutes.
Cool and cut into bars.

HAWAIIAN FRUIT BARS

Cook over low heat until thick and smooth:
2 cups dried apricots or apples, chopped
2 - 8 oz. cans crushed pineapple in juice
2 cups dates, chopped
3/4 cup apple juice or water

Remove from heat and add:
1 cup butter
1 tsp. vanilla   2 cups whole grain flour
1/3 cup rolled oats   1/3 cup oat bran
1 cup coconut   1/2 tsp. salt

   Combine and place in a greased 9 x 13" pan.
Bake at 350° F. for 30 minutes. Chill.

117

RAISIN MUMBLES

Beat:

¾ cup butter, melted   ¼ cup applesauce

Add:

1¾ cups whole grain flour   ½ tsp. salt
½ tsp. baking soda   1 cup rolled oats
½ cup oat bran   2 Tbsp. barley malt or
                                        ½ tsp. stevia

Press half of mixture into a greased 9 x 13" pan.

In saucepan mix:

2½ cups raisins   2 Tbsp. cornstarch
¾ cup apple juice or water   3 Tbsp. lemon juice

   Cook and cool.
Pour filling into pan and sprinkle remaining crumbs over top.
Bake at 400° F. for 20 - 30 minutes. Cool.

RAISIN MOLASSES BARS

Bring to a boil:

2½ cups raisins   ½ cup apple juice or water

   Remove from heat.

Sprinkle over raisins:

5 tsp. baking soda

Add:

1 cup butter

In mixer bowl:

3 eggs   5½ cups whole grain flour
½ cup molasses   ½ cup oat bran

   Beat eggs and molasses. Add flour, bran, and raisin mixture. Mix until just combined.
Pat into a greased jelly roll pan. With hands, smooth a beaten egg white over top.
Bake 350° F. for 20 - 30 minutes.

Note: Some hypoglycemics and diabetics will need to go easy with these! Save them for special occasions.

MONKEY BARS

1 cup butter, melted
2 eggs
2 cups bananas, mashed
1 tsp. vanilla
2 cups whole grain flour
1/4 cup barley malt or 1 tsp. stevia

1 cup shredded coconut
1/2 cup oat bran
2 1/2 tsp. baking powder
1 tsp. cinnamon
2/3 cup walnuts, chopped

Beat liquid ingredients together. Add rest of ingredients in order given. Spread in greased jelly roll pan.
Bake 350° F. for 25 - 30 minutes.

PEANUT BUTTER BARS

1/2 cup butter, melted
1/2 cup applesauce
1 cup peanut butter
2 eggs
2 tsp. vanilla
1/3 cup barley malt or 1 1/4 tsp. stevia, opt.

2 cups whole grain flour
1 cup rolled oats
1/2 tsp. salt
2 tsp. soda
2 tsp. baking powder
1 cup carob chips

Cream liquid ingredients. Add rest of ingredients and mix until just combined. Press into a greased jelly roll pan.
Bake 350° F. for 25 minutes. Cool 10 minutes and cut into bars.

PEANUT BUTTER OATMEAL BARS

1/2 cup butter
1/2 cup applesauce
1 cup peanut butter
2 eggs
1 tsp. vanilla
3 Tbsp. frozen white grape juice conc.
1/4 cup barley malt or 1 tsp. stevia

2 cups whole grain flour
1 1/2 cups rolled oats
1/2 cup oat bran
1 tsp. baking soda
1 tsp. salt
1/2 cup apple juice

Cream ingredients in first column. Add rest of ingredients and mix until just moistened. Spread on a greased jelly roll pan.
Bake at 350° F. for 25 minutes.

Opt: Spread with Carob Peanut Butter Frosting on top *(page 106)*. Chill.

RAISIN BARS

In a saucepan, cook 3 minutes:

1 cup raisins   ½ cup apple juice

Remove from heat and add:

¼ cup butter

In mixer bowl:

1 egg   ¾ cup applesauce
2 Tbsp. barley malt or ½ tsp. stevia, opt.   1 cup whole grain flour
1 tsp. cinnamon   ¼ tsp. nutmeg
1 tsp. baking soda   ¼ tsp. vanilla
½ cup chopped nuts

   Mix all ingredients together, adding raisins last. Spread in a greased 8 x 8" pan. Bake 350° F. for 30 - 35 minutes.

ZUCCHINI BARS

3 eggs, beaten   2 cups zucchini, grated
1 cup olive oil   ½ cup oat bran
½ cup barley malt or 2 tsp. stevia, opt.   1½ cups whole grain flour
2 tsp. baking soda   1 tsp. baking powder
1 Tbsp. cinnamon   1 tsp. salt, scant

   Mix all together. Pour into a greased 9 x 13" pan.
Bake at 350° F. for 30 - 35 minutes. Cool.
If desired, frost with any cream cheese icing *(pages 105 or 106)*.

APPLESAUCE COOKIES

1 cup butter, softened   2 tsp. cinnamon
2 eggs   ½ tsp. cloves
½ cup barley malt or 1½ tsp. stevia   ¼ tsp. salt
2 cups applesauce   1 tsp. nutmeg
4 cups oat bran   2½ tsp. baking soda
2 cups whole grain flour   1 cup raisins

   Beat wet ingredients together. Add rest of ingredients and beat until just combined.
Drop by spoonfuls onto cookie sheet. Flatten slightly.
Bake at 375° F. for 18 - 20 minutes.   Yield: 3 dozen

APPLESAUCE CAROB CHIP COOKIES

2 eggs
1 cup butter, melted
2 cups applesauce
5 cups whole grain flour
1 cup oat bran
1 Tbsp. cinnamon
2 tsp. baking powder

2 tsp. baking soda
2 tsp. salt
1/4 cup barley malt or
    1 tsp. stevia
1 cup carob chips or raisins
1/2 cup chopped nuts

Mix wet ingredients, then add rest of ingredients and mix until just combined. Drop by spoonfuls onto cookie sheet. Flatten slightly. Bake at 350° F. for 15 - 20 minutes.   Yield: 3 dozen

Note:
    Most sugar free cookies taste best when cold.

BANANA CAROB CHIP COOKIES

In mixer bowl, beat:
1/2 cup butter, melted
4 eggs

1/2 cup olive oil

Add:
2 cups mashed bananas, very ripe
1/4 cup barley malt or 1 tsp. stevia, opt.

5 tsp. baking soda
2 tsp. vinegar

Mix again.

Add and mix:
5 cups whole grain flour
1 tsp. cinnamon
1/4 tsp. cloves

1 tsp. salt
1 tsp. nutmeg

Stir in:
1 cup carob chips

1 cup chopped nuts

Drop by spoonfuls on cookie sheet and flatten slightly. Bake 350° F. for 12 minutes.   Yield: 5 dozen

BANANA OATMEAL COOKIES (EGG FREE)

Tip:

Dark cookie sheets and heavily greased sheets cause cookies to burn on the bottom and edges.

Combine:

3 mashed bananas

2 Tbsp. barley malt or 1/2 tsp. stevia, opt.

1/3 cup olive oil

1 tsp. vanilla

Stir in:

1 1/2 cups rolled oats

1/2 cup oat bran

1 cup chopped walnuts

1/2 cup whole grain flour

1/2 tsp. baking soda

1/4 cup raisins

Drop by spoonfuls on cookie sheet. Flatten lightly with fork. Bake 350° F. for 15 minutes.

SOFT CAROB COOKIES

1/2 cup butter, melted

2 eggs

2/3 cup carob powder

1/2 cup barley malt or 1 1/2 tsp. stevia, opt.

1/2 cup sour milk or apple juice

1 cup chopped nuts

1/2 cup applesauce

2 1/2 cups whole grain flour

1 tsp. salt

1 tsp. baking soda

2 tsp. vanilla

1/4 cup apple juice conc.

Mix all ingredients, folding nuts in last. Drop by spoonfuls onto cookie sheet.
Bake 375° F. for 10 - 12 minutes.

CAROB CHIP COOKIES

Our favorite!

1 cup butter, melted
4 large eggs
2 tsp. vanilla
¼ cup barley malt or 2 tsp. stevia, opt.
3 cups rolled oats
1 cup chopped nuts

2 cups whole grain flour
2 tsp. cream of tartar
2 tsp. baking soda
½ tsp. salt
1½ cups carob chips

Beat first 3 ingredients.
Add rest of ingredients and mix until just blended.
Do not overmix!
Drop by spoonfuls onto cookie sheet and flatten.
Bake 375° F. for 12 minutes.   Yield: 4 dozen cookies

CAROB NUT COOKIES

½ cup butter, melted
2 eggs
½ cup applesauce
¼ cup barley malt or 1½ tsp. stevia
⅔ cup carob powder
1 tsp. baking soda

2 tsp. vanilla
2½ cups whole grain flour
1 tsp. salt
¾ cup sour milk or apple juice
1 cup chopped nuts

Note:
Buttermilk and sour milk can be used interchangeably.
If you don't have any of either, make sour milk by putting 1 Tbsp. lemon juice in cup, and add milk to make 1 cup. Let set 5 minutes.

Beat butter, eggs, and applesauce together.
Add rest of ingredients in order given.
Fold in nuts last.
Drop by spoonfuls onto cookie sheet.
Bake 375° F. for 10 - 12 minutes.   Yield: 2 - 3 dozen cookies

CAROB SANDWICH COOKIES

Tip: Store whole grain flour in refrigerator or freezer.

For really fresh flour, you may want to invest in a grain mill. See "Resources" in the back of book for one source to buy from.

2 eggs
1 cup apple juice conc.
1/2 cup olive oil

3 1/3 cups whole grain flour
1 tsp. baking soda
2/3 cup carob powder

Mix wet ingredients together until well beaten. Add dry ingredients. Mix until just combined. Drop by spoonfuls on cookie sheet. Flatten into 1 1/2 - 2" rounds that are about 1/4" thick.
Bake at 350° F. for 9 - 12 minutes or until cookies feel dry. Remove cookies and allow to cool completely. Put bottoms of cookies together in pairs.
Fill with ice cream and freeze. (Soften in refrigerator 1 hour before serving) (or)

Fill with a thin layer of the following icing and refrigerate:
1 cup malt sweetened carob chips   1/3 cup peanut butter

Melt in double boiler, stirring constantly.

DATE OAT COOKIES

3/4 cup apple juice
1 cup chopped dates
1/2 cup butter
2 eggs
2 tsp. vanilla
1 1/2 cups whole grain flour
2 cups rolled oats
1/2 cup oat bran
2 Tbsp. barley malt or 3/4 tsp. stevia, opt.
1 1/2 tsp. baking soda
1/2 tsp. salt
1 cup chopped walnuts

Cook juice and dates together 3 minutes. Add butter and set aside. Beat eggs and add rest of ingredients. Mix until just combined. Drop by teaspoonfuls onto cookie sheet.
Bake 350° F. for 15 - 18 minutes.   Yield: 3 - 4 dozen cookies

DEBBIE COOKIES

1 cup butter, melted
4 eggs
1/2 cup applesauce
2 tsp. vanilla
2 cups whole grain flour
2 cups rolled oats
2 cups oat bran

1 tsp. salt
2 tsp. cinnamon
1/2 tsp. nutmeg
1 1/2 tsp. baking soda
1/2 tsp. cream of tartar
1/2 cup barley malt or
       1 tsp. stevia

Mix wet ingredients. Add rest of ingredients in order given. Do not overmix. Let set several hours or overnight in refrigerator. Shape into flat round cookies.
Bake 375° F. for 12 - 15 minutes. Cool.
Put 2 cookies together with Decorating Icing or Boiled Flour Icing
(page 104 or 105).

CLARA'S COOKIES

Simmer 3 minutes:
1 1/2 cups apple juice
1/2 cup dried or raw apples, diced

1/2 cup raisins
1/2 cup date pieces

Beat:
1/4 cup butter
2 eggs

1/4 cup applesauce
1 tsp. vanilla

Add:
1 cup rolled oats
1/2 cup oat bran
1/2 tsp. cinnamon

1 cup whole grain flour
1 tsp. baking soda
1/2 cup chopped nuts

Mix until just combined.
Refrigerate 1 hour. Drop by spoonfuls onto greased cookie sheet.
Bake 350° F. for 12 minutes.   Yield: 2 dozen cookies

Tip:
    Store cookies as soon as they are cooled to keep soft cookies soft, and crisp cookies crisp.

GOLDEN COOKIES

Tip: For a sweeter finished product, in recipes calling for fruit juice, you can substitute frozen concentrate in place of the juice.

Beat:
1/4 cup butter, melted
2 eggs

1 cup mashed pumpkin
1/4 cup apple juice conc.

Add:
2 cups whole grain flour
1/2 cup wheat germ
1/2 tsp. cinnamon
1/2 tsp. nutmeg
1/4 cup barley malt or 1 tsp. stevia

1/2 tsp. salt
1 1/2 tsp. baking soda
3/4 cup milk or apple juice
1/2 cup chopped walnuts
1 cup raisins

Mix and drop by spoonfuls onto cookie sheet.
Bake 350° F. for 12 - 15 minutes.

Yield: 3 dozen cookies

DATE DROP COOKIES

For guests and special occasions.

In blender:
1 1/2 cups dates
2 tsp. vanilla

2 eggs

Process until smooth. Pour into mixer bowl.

Add:
1/2 cup butter, melted
1/4 cup oat bran
1 tsp. baking soda
1/2 cup raw sunflower seeds
1/4 cup carob chips

1/4 cup whole grain flour
1 cup rolled oats
1/2 cup raisins
1/2 cup chopped pecans

Mix and drop by spoonfuls onto greased cookie sheet.
Bake at 350° F. for 15 - 20 minutes.   Yield: 1 1/2 dozen cookies

MOLASSES COOKIES

Cream:

³/₄ cup butter

2 Tbsp. barley malt or ¹/₂ tsp. stevia, opt.

1 egg

¹/₄ cup molasses

Add:

2 cups whole grain flour

1 tsp. cinnamon

¹/₂ tsp. ginger

2 tsp. baking soda

¹/₂ tsp. cloves

¹/₂ tsp. salt

Mix. These work great for cutout cookies; or shape into balls and press onto cookie sheet.
Bake 375° F. for 10 - 12 minutes.

BANANA OATMEAL COOKIES

Beat together:

1 egg

2 Tbsp. barley malt or ¹/₂ tsp. stevia, opt.

1 cup mashed bananas

³/₄ cup applesauce

Add:

1¹/₂ cups whole grain flour

¹/₂ tsp. baking soda

¹/₂ tsp. nutmeg

¹/₄ cup oat bran

1 tsp. salt

³/₄ tsp. cinnamon

1¹/₂ cups rolled oats

¹/₂ cup chopped nuts

Mix until just combined.
Drop by spoonfuls onto cookie sheet.
Bake 350° F. for 15 minutes.

ADA'S OATMEAL FRUIT COOKIES

In saucepan, combine and bring to a boil:

1 cup dates
1 1/2 cups apple juice

1 cup raw apples, diced

In mixer bowl, combine:

2 well beaten eggs
1 cup whole grain flour
1/2 cup oat bran
1 tsp. baking soda
1/2 tsp. cinnamon
1/2 cup chopped nuts

1 tsp. vanilla
1 1/2 cups rolled oats
2 Tbsp. apple juice conc.
1 tsp. baking powder
3/4 cup olive oil

Add fruit.

Let set 10 minutes to absorb moisture.
Drop by teaspoonfuls onto cookie sheet.
Bake 375° F. for 20 minutes or until brown.   Yield: 3 dozen cookies

OATMEAL RAISIN COOKIES

Combine in saucepan:

1 1/2 cups raisins

1 1/4 cups apple juice

Bring to a boil and cook 3 minutes.

Stir in:

1/3 cup butter

In mixer bowl:

2 eggs, beaten
1/2 cup barley malt or 2 tsp. stevia, opt.
1 cup rolled oats
1/2 tsp. nutmeg
1/2 tsp. salt
1/2 cup chopped nuts

2 1/2 cups whole grain flour
1/2 cup oat bran
2 tsp. cinnamon
1 tsp. baking powder
1 tsp. baking soda

Add raisins and mix until just combined.
Drop by spoonfuls onto cookie sheet.
Flatten slightly.
Bake 350° F. for 15 minutes.   Yield: 1 1/2 dozen cookies

PEANUT BUTTER COOKIES

Beat:

½ cup butter, melted
½ cup barley malt or 2 tsp. stevia
1¼ cups peanut butter
1 tsp. vanilla

½ cup applesauce
3 eggs
1 Tbsp. olive oil

Add:

2½ cups whole grain flour
1 tsp. baking powder
½ tsp. cream of tartar

½ tsp. salt
2 tsp. baking soda

Mix until just combined. Drop onto cookie sheet. Flatten with a fork in criss-cross style.
Bake 350° F. for 12 minutes.

SOFT PEANUT BUTTER COOKIES

In a small saucepan, cook:

½ cup apple juice concentrate

½ cup dates

Add:

½ cup butter

In mixer bowl, combine:

1½ cups peanut butter
2 tsp. vanilla
½ cup oat bran

2 eggs
2 cups whole grain flour
1 tsp. baking soda

Add date mixture and mix until just combined. Drop by teaspoonfuls onto baking sheet. Flatten with a fork in criss-cross style.
Bake 375° F. for 12 minutes.   Yield: 3 dozen cookies

PEANUT BUTTER CAROB CHIP COOKIES

Hint:
Remove cookies from cookie sheet immediately after removing from oven.

Cream:

1/2 cup butter, softened
4 Tbsp. apple juice concentrate

1 cup peanut butter
1/2 cup applesauce

Add:

2 eggs, beaten
1 tsp. vanilla
2 cups whole grain flour
1/2 tsp. cream of tartar
1/4 cup barley malt or 1 tsp. stevia, opt.

1 tsp. baking soda
1 cup rolled oats
1 cup carob chips
1 cup chopped nuts

Mix until just combined. Drop by spoonfuls onto baking sheet.
Bake 375° F. for 15 minutes.   Yield: 3 dozen cookies

PECAN SANDIES
(Pictured on front cover)

Beat together:

1/2 cup butter, melted
1/3 cup barley malt or 1 tsp. stevia
1 tsp. vanilla

1/2 cup olive oil
2 eggs

Add:

1 1/2 cups whole grain flour
1/2 cup oat bran
2 1/2 cups rolled oats
1/4 tsp. salt
1/8 tsp. cream of tartar

1/2 tsp. baking soda
1/2 tsp. cinnamon
3/4 cup pecans
1/2 cup raisins

Mix and drop by spoonfuls onto baking sheet.
Bake 350° F. for 20 minutes.   Yield: 2 dozen cookies

PUMPKIN EATER'S BARS

Crust:

³/₄ cup butter
1¹/₄ cups whole grain flour
¹/₂ tsp. salt

1¹/₂ cups rolled oats
¹/₂ cup chopped nuts
¹/₂ tsp. baking soda

   Mix until crumbly. Reserve 1¹/₂ cups. Press remaining crumbs onto greased 8 x 12" pan.
Bake 375° F. for 10 minutes.

Filling:
In blender, mix:
16 oz. pumpkin
2 Tbsp. barley malt or ¹/₂ tsp. stevia
2 tsp. cinnamon
¹/₄ tsp. nutmeg

²/₃ cup milk
1 egg
¹/₄ tsp. ginger

   Spread over baked crust.
Sprinkle remaining crumb mixture over filling.
Bake 20 - 25 minutes.
Chill. Cut into bars.
Opt: Top with whipped cream.

TROPICAL COOKIES (EGG FREE)

¹/₂ cup butter, melted
1 cup crushed pineapple, with juice
¹/₂ cup orange juice conc.
2 cups whole grain flour

1 cup shredded coconut
¹/₄ cup oat bran
¹/₂ tsp. baking soda

   Combine ingredients in order given.
Bake 350° F. for 20 minutes.

Yield: 3 dozen cookies

WALNUT YOGURT COOKIES

1/2 cup butter, softened
2 eggs
1 Tbsp. lemon juice
1 Tbsp. frozen orange juice conc.
1/4 cup barley malt or 1 tsp. stevia, opt.

1/2 cup yogurt
2 1/2 cups whole grain flour
1 tsp. baking soda
1 cup walnuts, chopped

Mix ingredients in order given. Drop by spoonfuls onto cookie sheet.
Bake 350° F. for 15 minutes.

Yield: 2 dozen cookies

WHOOPIE PIES

1 1/2 cups butter
6 eggs
1 Tbsp. baking soda dissolved in:
        1 cup hot apple juice
1 1/2 tsp. vanilla
1 1/2 cups sour milk (or) apple juice

4 cups whole grain flour
1 1/2 cups carob powder
2 cups rolled oats
1/2 cup oat bran
1 1/4 tsp. salt
2 Tbsp. barley malt or
        3/4 tsp. stevia, opt.

Mix together and let set 1/2 hour. Drop by teaspoonfuls onto greased baking sheet. Flatten.
Bake 350° F. for 10 - 12 minutes.
Cool. Sandwich cookies, bottom sides together with Boiled Flour Icing *(page 104)*.

BANANA WHOOPIE PIES

Beat together:
2 eggs
3/4 cup olive oil

2 cups mashed bananas
1 tsp. vanilla

Add:
3 1/4 cups whole grain flour
2 tsp. baking soda
1 tsp. cinnamon

1/4 cup oat bran
1/2 tsp. salt

Mix together. Drop by teaspoonfuls on cookie sheet.
Bake 350° F. 12 minutes. When cool, sandwich bottoms together with Boiled Flour Icing *(page 104)*.

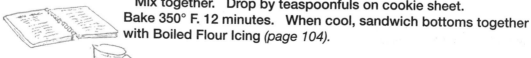

PUMPKIN WHOOPIE PIES

Beat together:

1½ cups cooked mashed pumpkin
2 eggs
½ cup applesauce
¼ cup barley malt or 1 tsp. stevia, opt.

1 Tbsp. apple juice conc.
½ cup olive oil
1 tsp. vanilla

Stir in:

3 cups whole grain flour
1 tsp. ginger
1 tsp. baking powder
1 tsp. baking soda

1½ tsp. cinnamon
½ tsp. cloves
1 tsp. salt

Mix until just combined.
Drop by heaping teaspoonfuls on greased cookie sheet.
Flatten slightly.
Bake 350° F. for 15 minutes.
When cool, sandwich cookies, bottom sides together with Boiled
Flour Icing *(page 104)*.

ZUCCHINI COOKIES

Beat together:

¾ cup butter, softened

1 egg

Add, and mix together:

2 cups whole grain flour
¼ tsp. salt
½ cup barley malt or 1¾ tsp. stevia, opt.

1 tsp. baking powder
1 tsp. vanilla

Fold in:

1 cup shredded zucchini
½ cup carob chips

Drop by spoonfuls onto greased baking sheet.   Flatten.
Bake 350° F. for 15 minutes.

133

Desserts

APPLE CRISP

Slice peeled apples into an 8 x 12" pan.

Sprinkle over apples:
2 Tbsp. apple juice   cinnamon

Topping:
3/4 stick butter   1 cup oatmeal
1 cup whole grain flour   1/2 cup bran
1/4 cup chopped nuts   1 tsp. barley malt or 1/4 tsp.
                                                                           stevia

Mix together with a fork.
Sprinkle over apples.
Bake 350° F. for 30 - 35 minutes.

In a hurry? Sprinkle topping over 2 qts. Apple Pie Filling.
Bake as usual.

Time Saver:
When you are using a tried and proven yummy recipe - make a double batch. Freeze half for those busy times you don't have time to cook or bake.

PEAR CRISP

Follow apple crisp recipe except:
Use pears instead of apples.
Sprinkle 1 Tbsp. minute tapioca over the pears and stir.
Sprinkle cinnamon over top.
Sprinkle crumb topping over pears and bake.

APPLE CRISP (FAT FREE)

Stir together in 2 quart baking pan:
6 medium apples, peeled and chopped
1/2 cup frozen apple juice conc.   1 Tbsp. lemon juice
3/4 tsp. cinnamon   1/4 tsp. nutmeg
1/2 cup raisins   1/4 cup chopped dates

Topping:
1 cup rolled oats   1/4 cup bran
1/4 cup chopped nuts   2 Tbsp. date sugar, opt.
2 Tbsp. frozen apple juice concentrate

Stir together and sprinkle over apples.
Bake covered 350° F. for 30 minutes.
Remove cover and bake an additional 10 minutes or until lightly browned.

137

APPLE DUMPLINGS

Pastry:
Beat:
¹/₂ cup butter, softened   1 egg
4 oz. cream cheese, room temp.   1 Tbsp. vinegar

Add:
1 tsp. baking powder   ¹/₂ tsp. salt
2³/₄ cups whole grain flour

   Cut 4 apples in half. Peel and core. Divide pastry in 4 equal parts and roll each piece out in a circle big enough to wrap an apple, approximately 8" in diameter. Brush melted butter on pastry then sprinkle cinnamon and date sugar on top. Place 2 halves in middle of circle, centers together like a whole apple, and form pastry around apples. Place in baking pan. Brush tops with egg white and sprinkle with cinnamon.
Bake 375° F. for 50 minutes. Serve hot with milk, ice cream, or applesauce.

Note: Try filling apple cavities with raisins. Yummy!

RASPBERRIES 'N DUMPLINGS
Delicious!

Hint:
   For a sweeter finished product:
   In recipes calling for fruit juice, substitute frozen concentrate instead.

In a pan, bring to a boil:
1¹/₂ cups apple juice   2 Tbsp. butter, opt.
1 pint black raspberries or blackberries

Dumplings:
2 Tbsp. butter, melted   1 cup whole grain flour
1¹/₂ tsp. baking powder   ¹/₈ tsp. salt
³/₄ tsp. vanilla   ¹/₃ cup milk or fruit juice

   Stir together and drop dumplings in sauce. Cover and simmer 20 minutes. Serve warm or cold.

APPLE TORTE

Cook, stirring constantly, until thickened:

1²/₃ cups apple juice   3 Tbsp. cornstarch

Add:

1 tsp. vanilla   1 Tbsp. butter

Crumble together:

2 cups whole grain flour   1 cup rolled oats
½ cup oat bran   1 cup butter, softened

Press half of crumbs in a 9 x 13" pan.

Cover with:

4 cups sliced apples

Sprinkle cinnamon over apples. Pour cooked mixture over apples. Cover with remaining crumbs.
Bake 350° F. for 30 minutes.

Hint:
Be sure to use ripe, sweet apples for apple recipes.

RHUBARB CRUNCH

½ cup butter, melted   ½ cup olive oil
2 cups whole grain flour   1 cup rolled oats
½ cup oat bran   2 tsp. cinnamon
¼ cup barley malt or 1 tsp. stevia, opt.

Mix above ingredients. Pat half of crumbs into greased 8 x 12" pan.

Layer onto crumbs:

4 - 6 cups diced rhubarb

Combine in small saucepan:

1 cup frozen apple juice conc.   4 Tbsp. cornstarch
1 cup apple juice   2 tsp. vanilla

Bring to a boil. Cook 2 - 3 minutes. Pour over rhubarb. Top with remaining crumbs.
Bake 350° F. for 45 minutes or until rhubarb is tender.

CHERRY CHEESECAKE

Crust:

$^3/_4$ stick butter, melted   1 cup rolled oats
1 cup whole grain flour

Mix and press into 9 x 13" pan.

Filling:

4 eggs, beaten   2 tsp. whole grain flour
4 tsp. lemon juice
2 - 8 oz. pkgs. Philadelphia cream cheese

Blend together and pour over crust.
Bake 300° F. for 1 hour and 15 minutes. Cool. Top with cherry filling.

Cherry filling:

1 quart sour cherries $^1/_2$ cup apple juice
$^1/_2$ cup apple juice concentrate   4 Tbsp. cornstarch
cinnamon

Stir cornstarch into juice. Stir into boiling cherries and concentrate.   Stir until boiling and thickened.

SOUR CHERRY DESSERT

In medium saucepan, bring to a boil:
3 cups sour cherries

Add:

3 Tbsp. cornstarch dissolved in:
$^1/_4$ cup thawed apple or white grape juice concentrate

Stir constantly, allowing to boil 1 - 2 minutes.

Add:

1 tsp. cinnamon $^1/_8$ tsp. salt
1 Tbsp. barley malt or $^1/_2$ tsp. stevia, opt.

Set aside.

(More on next page.)

Tip:

Milk, egg, and cheese desserts can be used to good advantage with low calorie or light meals. A roast beef and mashed potato meal doesn't need a heavy dessert like cheesecake.

Mix batter in mixer bowl:

1 cup butter
4 eggs, beaten
4 Tbsp. barley malt or 1 tsp. stevia
1 tsp. vanilla

1 tsp. salt
3 cups whole grain flour
1½ tsp. baking powder

Combine all ingredients in order given and mix. Set aside 1¾ cups batter. Spread batter in greased 9 x 13" pan. Spread cherry filling over batter. Spread 1¾ cups reserved batter over all. Bake 350° F. for 40 minutes.

Note: Also good with apple pie filling.

CHERRY DELIGHT

CRUST:

¾ stick butter, melted
1 cup whole grain flour

1 cup rolled oats

Press into 8 x 12" pan. Microwave 3 minutes or bake 375° F. for 12 minutes.   Allow to cool.

TOP CHERRY LAYER:

In kettle, bring to a boil:
1 quart sour cherries

Combine and stir into boiling cherries:
2 rounded Tbsp. cornstarch dissolved in:
          ½ cup thawed apple juice concentrate
1 tsp. cinnamon

Stir 1 - 2 minutes while boiling. Set aside.

MIDDLE LAYER:

In mixer bowl, combine:
½ pint heavy whipping cream
1 Tbsp. white grape juice conc.

pinch salt
1 tsp. vanilla

Whip at high speed until soft peaks form.

Fold in:
8 oz. softened cream cheese, cut in slices

Whip until stiff peaks form. Spread over cooled crust. Spread cooled cherries over top. Chill.

LIGHT AS AIR FRUIT GELATIN

2 envelopes unflavored gelatin
1 cup pineapple juice
3 cups pineapple juice
3 - 4 cups diced fruit

Sprinkle gelatin over 1 cup pineapple juice.
Stir constantly over medium heat until completely dissolved.
Add 3 cups of juice.
Chill until very thick.
Beat until frothy.
Add fruit. Fruit cocktail or any canned or frozen fruit may be used.
Do not use fresh or frozen pineapple, mangoes, papayas, or figs.
They contain an enzyme that keeps gelatin from setting.
Chill until set.

Note: Try other juices such as grape, orange, fruit punch, etc.

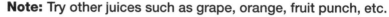

FRUIT PIZZA

Crust:
¹/₂ cup butter   1 egg

Cream together.

Add:
1¹/₃ cups whole grain flour   1 tsp. baking powder
pinch salt

Pat into greased pizza pan. Bake 375° F. for 10 minutes. Cool.

Cream together:
8 oz. cream cheese, softened
1 Tbsp. white grape juice concentrate

Spread over cooled crust.
Put fresh or canned fruit all around in circles, covering whole crust.
Use pineapple, peaches, pears, bananas, strawberries, blueberries, etc.
If desired spread the following glaze over fruit.

Cook until clear:
2 cups pineapple juice   2 Tbsp. gelatin

Allow to cool until slightly thickened.

Pour over pizza. Refrigerate.

STRAWBERRY DREAM
A dessert you can serve to guests

Crust:

¹/₄ cup butter, softened
1 cup rolled oats
¹/₂ cup chopped nuts
¹/₂ tsp. cinnamon

¹/₂ cup olive oil
1 cup whole grain flour
¹/₂ cup unsweetened coconut
¹/₄ tsp. salt

   Mix together and press into 9 x 13" pan.
Bake 350° F. for 10 minutes.

In blender, mix:
3 cups milk
1.5 oz. box sugar free vanilla pudding

Add:
8 oz. cream cheese, softened

   Blend again and pour over cooled crust.

In saucepan, bring to a boil:
2 cups water or pineapple juice

Dissolve:
0.6 oz. box sugarfree strawberry jello in:
                    2 cups juice or cold water
Stir in:
1 quart fresh or frozen strawberries, halved

   Cool. Pour on top. Chill.

Opt: Try other fruits:
          Peaches and orange jello
          Raspberries and raspberry or strawberry jello
          Sour cherries and cherry jello

Note: Gelatin may be used unstead of jello. Use pineapple juice
and 2 Tbsp. gelatin.

> **Note:** Sugar free jel-lo does not dissolve very well in boiling liquid. Always reserve part of the liquid in a cup and sprinkle jello over. Allow to dissolve for 3 - 5 minutes. Then stir into boiling liquid.

DATE PUDDING
(Pictured on front cover)

A favorite holiday dessert for guests!

1 cup chopped dates
1 tsp. baking soda
1 cup boiling water
2 eggs

1 Tbsp. butter
1½ cups whole grain flour
1 pinch salt
½ cup chopped walnuts

Put soda over dates. Pour boiling water over. Let set until cooled, then add rest of ingredients. Pour into greased 8 x 12" pan. Bake 375° F. for 25 minutes. Cool.

PUDDING AND CREAM:

Whip:
½ pint whipping cream
½ tsp. vanilla

1 pinch salt
1 Tbsp. apple juice conc.

In blender, mix:
1 small box instant butterscotch sugarfree pudding according to package directions.

At lowest speed on mixer, mix pudding into cream.

Place in layers in serving dish:
date cake, cut up in small squares
2 - 3 bananas
pudding and cream mixture (ending with pudding and cream
mixture on top)

Top with:
chopped nuts sprinkled over.

PEACH BANANA BREAD PUDDING

In large bowl, combine:
8 slices whole grain bread, cut into 1-inch cubes (approx. 3½ cups)
½ cup thawed apple juice or white grape juice concentrate
1 - 16 oz. can peaches, drained and chopped
1½ cups milk or fruit juice   4 eggs, lightly beaten
2 ripe bananas, sliced   1 tsp. lemon juice
1¼ tsp. cinnamon   ¼ tsp. nutmeg
1 tsp. vanilla

Mix well. Pour into greased 8 x 12" baking dish.
Bake at 325° F. for 60 - 65 minutes, or until a knife comes out
clean. Cool slightly. Serve warm or cold.   Serves 9

Need just a squeeze of lemon? Prick the lemon deeply with a fork, and squeeze the juice out - the lemon stays fresh longer than when it is cut.

RHUBARB PUDDING

3 cups chopped rhubarb   3 Tbsp. whole grain flour
1 Tbsp. frozen apple juice conc. 2 Tbsp. barley malt or
                                            ½ tsp. stevia
Mix above ingredients and place in greased 8 x 12" pan.

Mix:
½ cup butter   1 cup rolled oats
1 cup whole grain flour   ½ cup oat bran
¼ cup applesauce   ¼ cup chopped nuts
2 Tbsp. date sugar, opt.

Spread over rhubarb mixture.

Bake 375° F. for 40 minutes. Serve with milk or applesauce.

RHUBARB TAPIOCA

3 cups pineapple juice
$\frac{1}{2}$ cup tapioca
4 cups rhubarb, diced
1 cup white grape juice or pineapple juice
1 - 0.3 oz. box sugarfree strawberry jello or 1Tbsp. gelatin
1 tsp. vanilla
10 oz. crushed pineapple, drained
$\frac{1}{4}$ tsp. salt

In kettle, soak tapioca in 3 cups pineapple juice while preparing rhubarb. Soften jello in 1 cup juice.
Cook tapioca and rhubarb until soft.
Remove from heat and add remaining ingredients.
Cool.

MINI PEARL TAPIOCA

$\frac{1}{2}$ cup mini pearl tapioca
$\frac{1}{2}$ cup fruit punch or any fruit juice or water
1 - 0.3 oz. sugarfree jello
1 Tbsp. gelatin
4 cups fruit punch or any fruit juice
$\frac{3}{4}$ tsp. salt

Soak tapioca in lukewarm water 10 - 15 minutes.
Pour excess water off.
Soften jello and gelatin in $\frac{1}{2}$ cup juice or water.
Set aside.
Bring 4 cups juice to a boil.
Add salt and tapioca.
Boil and stir until tapioca is clear.
Remove from heat and add jello and gelatin.
Stir until dissolved.
Cool.
Add fruit of your choice: peaches, grapes, bananas, pineapple, fruit cocktail, etc.

Ice Cream
and
Frozen Desserts

SALT

CAROB SHAKES

In blender, mix:
3 - 4 frozen bananas
3 Tbsp. frozen apple juice conc.
milk to fill pitcher

2 Tbsp. dates
2 Tbsp. carob powder

> **Sugar provides only calories!** No protein, no vitamins, no minerals. It causes tooth decay, obesity, vitamin deficiency, diabetes, and hyperactivity in children.

STRAWBERRY SHAKES

In blender, mix:
2 frozen bananas
3 Tbsp. frozen apple juice concentrate
water to fill pitcher

1 cup yogurt
1 quart frozen strawberries

YOGURT PEACH SHAKE

In blender, mix:
1 cup yogurt
1 tsp. vanilla
2 Tbsp. frozen orange juice conc.

$\frac{1}{2}$ cup milk
1 banana
1 quart frozen peaches

BERRY-BERRY SMOOTHIE

1 pint frozen raspberries
3 Tbsp. frozen apple juice conc.
12 fresh or whole frozen strawberries
water to fill pitcher

1 ripe banana
$\frac{1}{4}$ cup yogurt

Blend all together in blender until smooth.

ORANGE CREAMSICLES

Hint: For easy blend-
er cleanup:
    Immediately after
using, add a couple
drops dishwashing
soap and fill halfway
with hot water. Cover
and turn on for a mo-
ment. Rinse.

3 cups milk
1 tsp. vanilla
1½ cups orange juice concentrate
1 tsp. xanthan gum, opt.

  Mix in blender.
Freeze until slushy and almost frozen.
Blend again and pour into popsicle molds or small cups with a
popsicle stick inserted.
Freeze.

Crave sherbet? Serve in dishes after blending the second time.
This tastes a little like sherbet.

Variation: Purple grape juice concentrate may be used instead of
orange.

STRAWBERRY SPARKLE FREEZE

2 Tbsp. frozen apple juice concentrate
¾ cup whipping cream
pinch salt
1 - 8 oz. pkg. cream cheese
1 Tbsp. frozen apple juice concentrate
2 cups fresh or frozen strawberries, thawed
1 cup crushed pineapple, undrained

  Whip cream, concentrate, and salt until stiff peaks form.
Set aside.
Mix cream cheese and 1 Tbsp. concentrate until smooth.
Add fruit.
Mix lightly. Fold in whipped cream.
Pour into 6 - cup ring mold.
Freeze.
Unmold on lettuce leaves 1 hour before serving and refrigerate to
soften.

ICE CREAM [FOR 6 QUART FREEZER]

Soften:
3 Tbsp. plain gelatin in:
1/2 cup apple juice concentrate

Stir softened gelatin into:
1 1/2 cups boiling apple juice concentrate

Cool slightly.
Add:
2 quarts milk

Chill.

In blender:

6 eggs
1 Tbsp. vanilla
1 can evaporated milk

1/4 cup dates
1 Tbsp. xanthan gum, opt.
gelatin mixture

Ingredients below in your choice of flavors

Blend everything in small batches and pour into freezer can. Lastly, fill to 6 quarts with milk.

PICK YOUR FLAVOR:

- **Peach or berry:** 1 1/2 - 2 quarts pureed fruit, peaches or berries
- **Peanut Butter :** 1 1/2 cups peanut butter
- **Carob-Banana:** 1/2 cup carob powder and 2 bananas, fresh or frozen
- **Carob Chip:** 1 cup carob chips (do not blend)

NOTE: Company coming? Need something extra special?
Omit the gelatin, concentrate and xanthan gum.

Add:
2 large boxes sugarfree instant vanilla pudding and 1 of above variations if desired.
        (or)
Butterscotch: 2 large boxes sugarfree instant butterscotch pudding; omit variations.

> **Don't have an ice cream freezer?**
> You can still make your own ice cream even if you don't have an ice cream freezer.
> Pour the mixture into ice cube trays. Freeze 1 - 1 1/2 hours until mushy, or freeze overnight. Allow to slightly thaw for 1/2 hour at room temperature. Process in blender or beat in mixer until creamy.

Pies

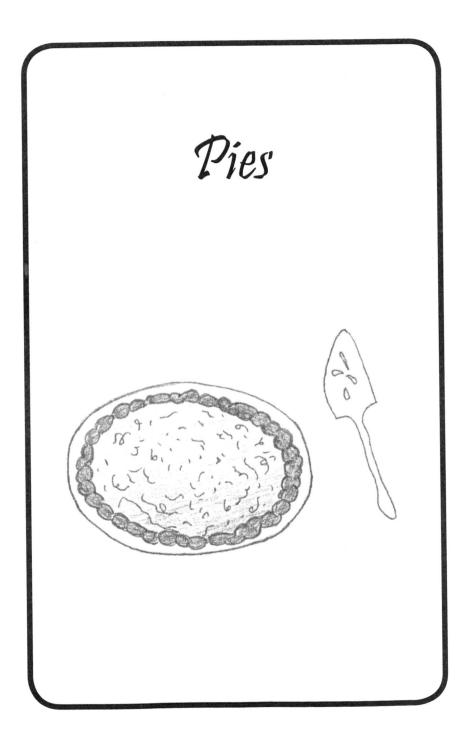

APPLE PIE

4 cups pared and sliced apples
1 - 12 oz. can frozen apple juice conc.
2 rounded Tbsp. minute tapioca
1 Tbsp. cornstarch

½ tsp. lemon juice
1 tsp. cinnamon
dash nutmeg

> **Hint:**
>   Egg white brushed on pie crust before adding filling keeps it from soaking.

   Stir all ingredients together in saucepan. Bring to a boil. Cook together 2 minutes. Pour into pie shell. Put on crumb topping. Bake 350° F. for 35 minutes.

CRAZY CRUST APPLE PIE

Combine:
1 egg
1 tsp. baking powder
⅔ cup olive oil

1 cup whole grain flour
½ tsp. salt
¾ cup apple juice

   Beat 2 minutes at medium speed. Pour batter into 9" pie pan. Pour 3 cups apple pie filling into center of batter. Do not stir. Bake 425° F. for 45 minutes.

BANANA CREAM PIE

2½ Tbsp. cornstarch
¼ tsp. salt
1 tsp. barley malt or ¼ tsp. stevia, opt.
2 eggs, beaten

2 cups milk
1 tsp. vanilla
3 bananas, sliced
1 baked pie shell

   Mix dry ingredients in saucepan. Add eggs and milk to dry ingredients. Cook until thick, stirring constantly. Add vanilla. Cool. Add bananas and pour into prebaked pie shell. Sprinkle coconut on top. **Note:** For a healthier, less refined pudding: use 1 Tbsp. cornstarch and 3 Tbsp. whole grain flour instead of 2½ Tbsp. cornstarch.

BLUEBERRY CHEESECAKE PIE

2 eggs
1/2 tsp. vanilla
1 - 8 oz. pkg. Philadelphia cream cheese

pinch salt
1/2 cup milk or apple juice
1 - 9" unbaked pie shell

Blend all ingredients together. Pour into pie shell.
Bake at 400° F. for 15 minutes. Reduce oven temperature to 325° F.
Continue baking 20 minutes.

2 cups blueberries
1 Tbsp. cornstarch

1/2 cup apple juice
2 Tbsp. apple juice
conc.

In saucepan, combine all ingredients.
Cook, stirring constantly, until clear and thickened.
Cool slightly.
Spoon over cream cheese mixture.
Chill.

CRANBERRY APPLE PIE

In blender, chop:
1 - 12 oz. can apple juice conc.
1 1/4 cups cranberries

1 Tbsp. cornstarch

Pour into saucepan.

Add:
4 cups pared, sliced apples
2 rounded Tbsp. minute tapioca
dash nutmeg

1/2 tsp. lemon juice
1 tsp. cinnamon
pinch of salt

Stir together and bring to a boil.
Cook 2 minutes. Remove from heat.

Add:
2 tsp. maple flavor

1/2 cup chopped walnuts

Pour into unbaked pie shell. Sprinkle crumb topping over.
Bake 350° F. for 35 minutes.

Hint:
Cut center from a tin pie pan. Use the outside rim to cover pie crust while baking to keep from over browning.

GRAPE MERINGUE PIE

1⅓ cups grape juice (concentrated or steam method is sweetest)
2 egg yolks
1 Tbsp. barley malt or ½ tsp. stevia, opt.
4 Tbsp. cornstarch dissolved in:
                    ½ cup cold grape juice
2 Tbsp. butter
1 tsp. lemon juice

Tip:
      When rolling pie dough between 2 pieces of wax paper, lightly wet counter before putting first sheet down to prevent slipping.

   Bring first 3 ingredients to a boil. Stir cornstarch in. Boil 1 - 2 minutes. Add butter and lemon juice. Set aside to cool.

Beat until stiff:
2 egg whites
¼ tsp. cream of tartar

   Fold into cooled filling. Pour into 8" prebaked, cooled pie shell. Chill.

PEACH PIE

Crust:
1 stick butter, softened
1 cup whole grain flour
½ tsp. cinnamon

½ cup unsweetened coconut
½ cup walnuts

   Mix together and press into pie pan, saving a little to sprinkle over top of pie.

Filling:
3½ cups fresh peaches
1 rounded Tbsp. orange juice conc.

3 Tbsp. minute tapioca
1 tsp. lemon juice

   Bring to a boil and cook 1 - 2 minutes.
Pour into pie shell. Sprinkle reserved crumbs over top.
Bake 10 minutes at 425° F. Lower oven temperature to 350° F. and bake 25 minutes longer.

100 %
Whole
Grain

Note: For pear pie, substitute ½ cup apple juice concentrate for orange juice and lemon. Add 1 additional Tbsp. minute tapioca.

Using goat milk?

When heating goat milk, it tends to get a "goaty" taste.

Solution: When milking, cool milk fast; milk directly onto a container of ice in the milk bucket. (We use a quart size freezer box.) After milking, wash it and return to the freezer for the next milking.

Also: When heating milk, heat as rapidly as possible. Turn burner to medium - high to high, and stir constantly to keep from scorching.

Be sure milk is fresh. Old goat milk tastes "goaty".

PUMPKIN PIE

In blender, mix:
3 eggs
1 cup hot pumpkin
2 cups hot milk
1 Tbsp. whole grain flour
3 Tbsp. barley malt or ½ tsp. stevia
1 tsp. cinnamon
¼ tsp. nutmeg

Pour into pie shell.
Bake 400° F. for 10 minutes.
Lower oven temperature to 350° F. and bake 40 minutes longer.

SPICY PUMPKIN PIE

(For those allergic to eggs and milk)

1 envelope unflavored gelatin
½ cup white grape juice concentrate

Sprinkle gelatin over the concentrate.
Heat over medium heat, stirring constantly, until dissolved.
Remove from heat.

Add:
1 - 16 oz. can pumpkin
½ cup white grape or apple juice conc.
1 tsp. cinnamon
¼ tsp. nutmeg
dash ginger
1 Tbsp. barley malt or ¼ tsp. stevia, opt.
1 - 8" baked pie shell

Mix well until smooth.
Pour into prebaked pie shell.
Chill.

Tip:

Goat milk is easier to digest. Many people who are allergic to cow milk can tolerate goat milk.

RHUBARB BLUEBERRY PIE

2¹/₂ cups rhubarb
2 cups blueberries
¹/₄ cup apple juice
   Combine and cook fruit until boiling.

pinch salt
1 tsp. cinnamon

Tip:
   Chill pie dough for easier rolling.

Add:
4 Tbsp. cornstarch in:
³/₄ cup apple juice

   Stir while boiling for 2 minutes.
Pour into pie shell.

Topping:
5 Tbsp. butter
¹/₂ cup rolled oats
¹/₄ cup oat bran

¹/₂ cup whole grain flour
¹/₄ cup nuts

   Sprinkle over pie.
Bake 375° F. for 10 minutes.
Lower heat to 350° F. and bake for 35 minutes more.

SOUR CHERRY PIE

3¹/₂ cups sour cherries, with juice
¹/₂ cup white grape juice concentrate or water
2 Tbsp. clear jel or cornstarch
1 Tbsp. barley malt or ¹/₄ tsp. stevia, opt.
1 Tbsp. butter
cinnamon

Tip:
   Too much mixing makes pie dough tough.

   In saucepan bring cherries to a boil.
Meanwhile dissolve clear jel or cornstarch in juice,
then pour into boiling cherries.
Stir until thickened. Remove from heat.
Add sweetener and butter.
Allow to cool while making pie shell.
Pour into pie shell.
Sprinkle with cinnamon.
Put top crust on, or crumb topping.
Bake 375° F. for 35 minutes.

STRAWBERRY PIE

1 - 9" prebaked pie shell
2½ cups fresh or whole frozen strawberries
½ cup apple juice concentrate
3 Tbsp. cornstarch
1 cup crushed strawberries
dash salt

Spread whole strawberries in pie shell.
Dissolve cornstarch in apple juice.
Stir into boiling crushed strawberries. Add salt.
Pour over berries in shell. Cool.

Opt: Top with whipped cream to serve.

STRAWBERRY DREAM PIE

Combine, mixing until well blended:
1 - 8 oz. pkg. Philadelphia cream cheese
2 Tbsp. frozen grape juice concentrate
½ tsp. vanilla   dash nutmeg

Set aside.

Whip until stiff peaks form:
½ cup whipping cream   1 pinch salt

Fold into cream cheese mixture.

Fold into mixture:
1½ cups fresh strawberry slices

Spoon into 9" prebaked pie shell.
Chill several hours or overnight.
Garnish with additional strawberries if desired.

CRUMB TOPPING (FOR PIES)

¾ stick butter, softened   1 cup oatmeal
1 cup whole grain flour   ½ cup oat bran
¼ cup chopped nuts   2 tsp. barley malt or ¼ tsp.
                                                    stevia

Mix together with fork. Sprinkle over 2 pies and bake.

OAT BRAN PIE CRUST

1 cup whole grain flour
1/4 tsp. salt
4 Tbsp. water

1/2 cup oat bran
1/4 cup olive oil

Combine dry ingredients. Stir in oil.
Crumble by hand while adding water.
Form into a flattened ball.
Roll out between 2 sheets of wax paper.
Fit into 8 or 9" pie pan.
Bake crust 12 minutes at 375° F. or fill pie with pie filling and bake according to pie directions.

Hint: Try using cornstarch instead of flour for rolling out pie dough, ensuring a flakier pie crust since it takes less.

OATMEAL PIE CRUST

Blend in blender until finely chopped:
1 cup rolled oats
1/2 cup nuts
1/8 tsp. salt

1/4 cup oat bran
1/2 tsp. cinnamon

Pour mixture into bowl.

Add:
1/4 cup melted butter

Press mixture onto bottom and sides of 8" pie pan.
Bake 375° F. for 12 minutes.

PIE CRUST

Beat until smooth:
1 cup butter, softened
8 oz. cream cheese, room temp.

2 eggs
2 Tbsp. vinegar

Add:
2 tsp. baking powder
5 1/2 cups whole grain flour

1 tsp. salt

Mix by hand when stiff, but don't overmix.
If sticky, chill slightly.
Roll out on floured counter.
Fold in half and place in pie pan.
Unfold. Trim around edge of pan and flute edges.

Note: Freeze extra crusts in pie pans in plastic bags, unbaked, for quick pie making.

Miscellaneous

WHIPPED CREAM

½ pint heavy whipping cream   pinch salt
1 Tbsp. white grape juice concentrate   1 tsp. vanilla

Pour cream and salt into chilled bowl.
Beat at high speed until soft peaks form.
Add vanilla and juice.
Beat until stiff peaks form.
Refrigerate until ready to use.

Note: For variety, try other juice flavors.

HOMEMADE BUTTER   (IN THE BLENDER)

Use raw milk. Let sit in the refrigerator for a day or so until the cream rises to the top. Skim the cream off and let age another day in the refrigerator. (If cream is frozen and then thawed, it turns to butter fast.)

Pour cream into your blender until it is just a little over half full. Blend, turning motor on and off as it gets thicker and forms small grains (rich cream forms butter at once). The volume will increase until it almost fills the blender, then the little grains of butter will begin to separate from the buttermilk. Stop the blender and use a rubber scraper to help form the butter into lumps that can be removed.

Place butter in a bowl that has been scalded and rinsed with cold water. Pour off buttermilk through a small strainer to remove every bit of butter. Chill the buttermilk to drink, or for baking. With a rubber scraper, "work" the butter, smoothing, turning, and pressing until the buttermilk is worked out. Rinse in cold water and work again until water runs clear. Add about ¼ tsp. of salt for every pound of butter. Mix well. Store covered in refrigerator.

YOGURT

Hint:
Yogurt and fruit is the perfect high-nutrient, low-calorie dessert, and is very economical, especially when you make your own yogurt.

Preheat oven to 100° F., and place large mouth glass jar in oven to warm; or baby food jars can be used for individual servings. If using plain yogurt for starter, this can also be placed in the oven to warm. Or an electric yogurt maker may be used. You will need a glass candy thermometer to be sure temperature doesn't get too high or too low.

In a kettle, heat 1 qt. milk to 180° F. Cool in sink of cold water to 112° F. Spoon a little bit of milk into room temperature yogurt starter and stir. Starter can be bought at food co-ops or health food stores. If unavailable, use ½ cup plain yogurt with active yogurt and acidophilus cultures, available in large grocery stores. Gently stir starter into milk. Pour into warmed jar. Cover. Let stand in warm place 6 - 8 hours, until set. Leave in shortest time possible for a milder tasting yogurt.

Immediately place in refrigerator with lid partly off. Do not stir until cold. Cover tightly after it is cold. Reserve ½ cup for starter for next batch. This can be done several times until it becomes weak and you need to start with new starter. When you feel experienced at making it, a double batch can be made at one time.

Serve yogurt as a dessert, drink, or substitute for sour cream in casseroles, meats, or soups. To avoid curdling, 1 tsp. cornstarch per cup yogurt may be added, stirring yogurt into soup just before serving. Yogurt is not fattening and is easier to digest than milk. Try yogurt salad dressing. Drink a glassful for energy when tired. For soft cookies and cakes, add yogurt. For pie crusts, use yogurt for the liquid for a flakier crust.

For variety, add any frozen fruit juice concentrate, fruit, berries, or jam to the yogurt to serve.

When taking antibiotics, yogurt should also be eaten as it contains acidophilus. Acidophilus promotes healthy intestinal bacteria. Antibiotics destroy the good bacteria along with the bad.

Yogurt is very beneficial to those who have colon or intestinal disorders.

ITALIAN SEASONING

5 Tbsp. oregano
2 tsp. onion powder

2 tsp. basil
1 tsp. garlic powder

Cover and shake well to mix.

On a low salt diet?
Season foods with herbs and spices. Mrs. Dash is an excellent substitute.

SEASONING SALT

1/2 cup salt
1 tsp. paprika
1 Tbsp. celery salt

1/4 tsp. garlic powder
1 tsp. pepper
2 tsp. onion powder

Cover and shake well to mix.

SALT SUBSTITUTE   (LOW SALT)

1 tsp. chili powder
1 Tbsp. garlic powder
6 Tbsp. onion powder
1 tsp. oregano

3 Tbsp. paprika
2 Tbsp. pepper
1 Tbsp. poultry seasoning
2 Tbsp. dry mustard

Combine all ingredients, mixing well.   Place in salt shaker and use instead of salt.

Tip:
Did you know that chili powder usually has salt in it?

TACO SEASONING

Place in a one pint jar:
1/2 cup onion flakes
3 tsp. paprika
1/4 tsp. cayenne pepper

3 Tbsp. ground cumin
2 tsp. chili powder
1/2 tsp. garlic powder

Cover tightly and shake well to mix.   To season, use 2 - 3 Tbsp. of the mix and 1/2 cup water for each pound of meat or beans.

PLAY DOUGH

1 cup refined flour
1 Tbsp. oil
1 cup water
1/2 cup salt
2 tsp. cream of tartar
food coloring

Combine all ingredients in a saucepan.
Cook over medium heat, stirring constantly, until mixture forms a ball.
Knead until smooth.
Store in covered container.
It keeps longer in the refrigerator.
Allow to set at room temperature before playing with it.

GAK   (A UNIQUE KIND OF PLAY DOUGH)

In a bowl, stir:
1 1/2 cups cold water
16 oz. Elmer's glue
food coloring

In a large cup, combine:
1 cup cold water
3 Tbsp. borax

While stirring both mixtures, slowly pour from the cup into the bowl.
When thick, knead on a table for 5 - 10 minutes.
Now have fun with rolling pins and cookie cutters; make worms, ropes, fake foods.
Spread it out and hold it up to your mouth and blow a huge bubble.
Store in ziploc bag or tightly closed container at room temperature.

Snacks

SODA CRACKERS

Beat:
1/4 cup olive oil
1 egg

Add:
2 1/2 cups whole grain flour
1 1/2 tsp. salt
3/4 tsp. baking soda

Mix and add:
1/3 cup apple juice

Roll out as thin as possible on a large cookie sheet.
Cut and prick each cracker with a fork.
Bake 400° F. for 12 - 15 minutes.
Store at room temperature.

NUTRITIOUS SNACKS:
Raw kohlrabi or sweet potato with peanut butter: Slice thinly and cover with cold water in refrigerator at least 1 hour to crisp up. Drain. Spread with peanut butter.

VEGETABLE CRACKERS

1/4 cup butter, softened, (or) olive oil
1/2 tsp. baking soda
1/4 tsp. celery salt
2 Tbsp. carrot, finely grated
1 - 2 Tbsp. cold tomato juice or ketchup
1/2 cup grated cheese

1 cup whole grain flour
1/4 tsp. salt
1/2 tsp. parsley flakes
1 Tbsp. onion, chopped fine
dash red pepper

Mix all ingredients except juice until thoroughly combined.
Add juice a little at a time.
Roll out very thin.
Cut.
Bake at 350° F. for 20 - 25 minutes.
Store in a tight container at room temperature.

OAT BRAN CRACKERS

4 heaping Tbsp. apple juice conc.	$\frac{1}{3}$ cup olive oil
2 Tbsp. molasses	1 tsp. vanilla
2 - 2$\frac{1}{2}$ cups whole grain flour	$\frac{1}{2}$ cup oat bran
$\frac{1}{2}$ tsp. baking powder	$\frac{1}{2}$ tsp. baking soda
$\frac{1}{4}$ tsp. salt	1 tsp. cinnamon

Mix all ingredients together. Use hands to mix when dough gets too stiff. Add flour until dough is not sticky. Roll dough on greased cookie sheet, covering sheet completely. Use a pizza cutter or knife to cut in 2" squares, but do not separate.
Bake 300° F. for 20 minutes. Cool on cookie sheet.
May be stored at room temperature.

Note: Some hypoglycemics are not able to tolerate molasses. Substitute 1 Tbsp. maple flavor for molasses.

NUTRITIOUS SNACKS:
Celery or apples with peanut butter: Cut apple in half and core. Fill cavities of celery or apple halves with peanut butter.

CRISPY RICE SNACK

$\frac{1}{2}$ cup peanut butter	2 Tbsp. water
2 Tbsp. frozen apple juice concentrate	$\frac{1}{2}$ tsp. vanilla
$\frac{1}{2}$ cup chopped nuts	$\frac{1}{2}$ tsp. cinnamon
2 cups crisp brown rice cereal	

Mix all ingredients together except cereal in a bowl. Add cereal and stir gently. Form into walnut sized balls.

ENERGY BALLS (A GREAT PROTEIN SNACK)

In blender, chop:

1 cup raw sunflower seeds	$\frac{1}{4}$ cup raisins

Mix with:

1 Tbsp. oat bran	1 Tbsp. apple juice conc.
1 - 16 oz. jar crunchy peanut butter	

Mix with hands. Make small balls. Roll in coconut.

YUM YUM BALLS

4 oz. cream cheese, softened
1/2 cup shredded unsweetened coconut
1/4 cup sunflower seeds
4 Tbsp. peanut butter
1/4 cup oat bran
2 Tbsp. chopped nuts

Mix ingredients together. Shape into small balls and roll in additional coconut. Refrigerate.

Note: For variety, try adding wheat germ or carob powder.

PEANUT BUTTER BALLS

1 cup peanut butter
2 Tbsp. apple juice
1/4 cup oat bran
2 Tbsp. sesame seeds
1 tsp. vanilla
1/4 cup rolled oats
1/4 cup chopped nuts
2 Tbsp. coconut

Mix all together with a fork.

For variety, add one of the following:
1/2 cup carob chips
1/2 cup raisins
4 Tbsp. carob powder

Shape into small balls (about 1 rounded tsp. each). Keep refrigerated until ready to serve.

FINGER JELLO

Soften:
3 Tbsp. gelatin in:
1/2 cup grape juice concentrate

Stir into:
1 cup boiling grape juice concentrate

Pour into 9 x 13" pan. Chill to set. Cut into squares or shapes with cookie cutters.

Note: Grape juice canned with steamer method is good. Also try apple juice concentrate or cider.

SOFT PRETZELS

1¹/₂ cups warm apple juice concentrate (containing ascorbic acid)
4 tsp. yeast
1 tsp. salt
3¹/₂ cups whole grain flour

1 Tbsp. vinegar
1 cup oat bran
1 egg white

Topping: Optional
salt or sesame seeds

   Dissolve yeast in juice.
When bubbly add salt, vinegar, and 2 cups flour. Beat until smooth.
Work bran and flour in. Let rise 1 hour. Punch down.
Now is when the children have fun!
Divide the dough into 15 pieces.
Roll each one into a long rope.
Make pretzel shapes or anything they come up with: letters, hearts, animals, etc. Use water to glue 2 parts together.
Brush with beaten egg white. Sprinkle topping on if desired.
Allow to rise on baking sheet 15 - 20 minutes.
Bake 400° F. for 20 minutes.

TRAIL MIX

1¹/₂ cups roasted peanuts
¹/₄ cup raisins
¹/₄ cup chopped dates

¹/₂ cup raw sunflower seeds
¹/₄ cup carob chips

   Mix and enjoy!

Canning
and
Freezing

CANNING AND FREEZING
<u>Without Sugar</u>

APPLESAUCE
Follow these tips for a sweeter sauce:
- Leave peels on and cores in the apples to cook them.
- Use fall apples that are completely ripe.
- Grimes and Yellow Delicious taste the sweetest. (I can the one kind and freeze the other to keep the 2 kinds separate, and mix them when ready to serve.
- Runny applesauce will not taste as sweet as medium to thick sauce.
- If doing a large amount of sauce, keep cut apples in salty water until you are ready to cook them. It helps to sweeten them, and keeps them from turning brown.

APPLE CIDER
When cider is in season, can your own. It is sweeter and more concentrated.
- Simply boil cider for 10 minutes. Ladle into warm jars and seal; (or) pour into quart jars, seal, and cold pack for 20 minutes.
Use for recipes calling for apple juice, in place of milk in cold cereals, or dilute for babies to drink.

> **Hint:** Add a little vinegar to the water when washing sprayed fruits and vegetables to aid in spray and wax removal.

SYRUP (FOR CANNING ANY FRUIT)
- Use white grape juice, diluted, 2 parts juice to 1 part water.
- Try apple juice
- Peaches and pears are also good with diluted pineapple juice.
- If fruit is not very sweet, do not dilute juice.
- If you slice fruit into jars instead of halves, it tends to be sweeter because it is less diluted (more fruit goes in).

BERRIES (RASPBERRIES, BLACKBERRIES, BLUEBERRIES)
- Do not wash. Freeze in airtight bags or freezer boxes.

APPLE PIE FILLING (MAKES 7 QUARTS)

Blend in large kettle:

1 cup quick cooking tapioca	1 tsp. salt
2 tsp. cinnamon	$\frac{1}{4}$ tsp. nutmeg

Add:

2 - 12 oz. cans apple juice conc.   7 cups cider or apple juice
$\frac{1}{4}$ cup barley malt or 2 tsp. liquid stevia, opt.

Cook on med - hi heat. Stir until thickened and bubbly. Cook an additional 2 minutes.
(Speed up cooking time by soaking tapioca in a little of the cold cider for $\frac{1}{2}$ hour.)

Add:

3 Tbsp. lemon juice

Stir into 35 - 40 sliced and peeled sweet apples.

Cold pack 15 minutes at a rolling boil.

APPLE PIE FILLING   (MAKES 7 QUARTS)

7 cups cider or apple juice	3 Tbsp. lemon juice
1$\frac{1}{2}$ cups instant clear jel	1 tsp. salt
2 - 12 oz. cans apple juice conc.	1 Tbsp. cinnamon
$\frac{1}{4}$ cup barley malt or 2 tsp. liquid stevia, opt.	
5 apples per quart (35 apples)	

Put part of cider in blender. Mix dry ingredients in while blending. (Clear jel may not all fit in at once.) Stir into sliced apples. Spoon into jars just to neck. Cold pack 15 minutes at a rolling boil.

Note: Pie filling is good for pie, apple crisp, or apple coffee cake.

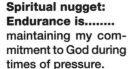

Spiritual nugget: Endurance is........ maintaining my commitment to God during times of pressure.

FRUIT SLUSH

2 - 6 oz. cans frozen white grape juice concentrate
3 cans water
1 - 20 oz. can crushed pineapple
1½ peck peaches or pears, sliced
10 ripe bananas, sliced
1 quart sliced strawberries, fresh or frozen

Mix all ingredients and freeze.
Allow to thaw slightly before serving.

TROPICAL FRUIT SLUSH

1 - 6 oz. can frozen orange juice concentrate
1½ cans water
8 ripe bananas, sliced
1 - 20 oz. can crushed pineapple
8 peaches, sliced
Strawberries may be added for color

Mix all ingredients and freeze. Allow to thaw slightly before serving.

BANANAS

Freeze for blender shakes or eating just so. Cut in half lengthwise. Spread out on cookie sheet until frozen. Store in plastic bag in freezer.

HOW TO PRESERVE A HUSBAND

Be careful in your selection; do not choose too young, and take only such as have been reared in a good moral atmosphere.

Some insist on keeping them in a pickle, while others keep them in hot water. This only makes them sour, hard, and sometimes bitter.

Even poor varieties may be made sweet, tender, and good, by garnishing them with patience, well sweetened with smiles of charity.

Keep warm with a steady fire of domestic devotion and serve with peaches and cream.

When thus prepared, they will keep for life.

JAM

(This jam uses "Pomona's Universal pectin" -
a 100% citrus Pectin. See page 202 for suppliers)

Bring to a boil:
6 cups mashed strawberries, raspberries, or blueberries
1 Tbsp. calcium water (included with pectin)

Meanwhile, mix together:
1 Tbsp. pectin powder
1 tsp. stevia

Add:
1/2 cup white grape juice concentrate

Mix well and stir into boiling fruit.
Stir vigorously 1 - 2 minutes to dissolve pectin.
Return to boiling and remove from heat.
Fill freezer containers.

Allow to cool. Freeze.

APPLE BUTTER

16 cups thick applesauce   2 Tbsp. cinnamon
2 cups cider or apple juice concentrate

Bake uncovered 350° F. for 3 hours or until the desired consistency, stirring occasionally. Pour in hot jars and seal.
Turn upside down until cooled.

Note: Save the pulp that comes out of the Victorio strainer. Put pulp through strainer again after you are done putting sauce through. Use this thick sauce for part or all of your apple butter.
Yield: 7 - 8 pints

Spiritual nugget:
What is done can never be undone, but what is broken can be fixed - by God's Grace!

PEAR BUTTER

1 cup frozen white grape juice conc.   12 cups pear sauce
1 Tbsp. cinnamon

Put in roaster and bake 350° F. for 3 hours, stirring occasionally.
Freeze or cold pack 20 minutes.

Note:
Raw pears may be pared and pureed in blender. Then follow recipe.

PICKLED BEETS

1½ cups vinegar
2½ cups white grape juice conc.
1 Tbsp. salt

1 tsp. allspice
1 Tbsp. cinnamon

   Select small young beets. Cook until tender.
Dip in cold water, peel off skin. Put beets in jars.
Make syrup with above ingredients. Boil 5 minutes.
Pour over beets.   Cold pack 15 minutes.
This is enough liquid for 3 - 4 quarts.

Note: If using larger beets, cut in chunks to put in jars.

MILLION DOLLAR PICKLES

4 quarts sliced cucumbers - ¼" thick slices
6 - 8 small onions, sliced in rings

Sprinkle over onions and cucumbers:
½ cup salt

   Cover with water - soak in this brine overnight.
Next morning, drain.
Pack cucumbers into jars.

Brine:

½ cup water
½ cup white grape juice concentrate
1 tsp. turmeric
1 Tbsp. mixed pickle spices

2¼ cups white vinegar
½ tsp. celery salt
2 Tbsp. white mustard seed

> **Spiritual nugget:**
>   **Freedom** is <u>not</u> the right to do what we want, but the power to do what we ought.

   Boil 1 - 2 minutes. Pour brine over cucumbers, filling jars to neck.
Put jars in canner. Bring to a boil.
Remove immediately.

SALT AND SUGAR-FREE PICKLES

Tip: Doing open kettle canning? (For anything except juices)

To ensure jars sealing, turn rings on tight and <u>immediately turn jars upside down</u> until cool.

Bring to a boil:

4½ cups white vinegar   14 cloves garlic
4½ cups water

Place in bottom of each jar:

1 grape leaf   3 whole peppercorns
1 strip horseradish, ½" x 3" long 1 tsp. mustard seed
1 whole clove

Fill each jar with cucumber strips.

Add :

2 sprigs of dill on top of each jar.
Pour on vinegar solution to within ¼" of top.
Put 2 cloves of the garlic in each jar.
Tighten lids and process in boiling water 15 minutes.   Yield: 7 pints

DILL PICKLES

Wash pickles and fill jars half full.
Add:

1 small clove garlic   1 sprig dill

Fill to top of jar with pickles.   Put grape leaf on top, pushing down around edge of jar.

Brine:

1 quart white vinegar   3 quarts hot water
1 cup salt

Bring to a boil and fill jars to the top.
Tightly seal.
Store in refrigerator or cold pack for 10 minutes.

RAINBOW PICKLE RELISH

Finely grind or process in blender:
20 large pickles (can substitute green tomatoes for part of pickles)
2 yellow or green peppers   2 red peppers
4 medium onions

Combine and soak for 1 hour in $\frac{1}{4}$ cup salt and water to cover.

Bring to a boil in a large pan:
$\frac{1}{2}$ cup frozen white grape juice conc.   1 Tbsp. celery seed
1 tsp. mustard seed   2 cups white vinegar
1 tsp. turmeric

Drain vegetables; add to syrup and heat. Simmer 10 minutes. Fill warm jars and seal.   Yield: 10 - 12 pints

ZUCCHINI RELISH

10 cups grated zucchini   2 cups white vinegar
$\frac{1}{2}$ cup grated carrot $\frac{1}{2}$ cup frozen white grape
2 cups chopped green peppers   juice conc.
2 cups chopped red peppers   1 tsp. turmeric
4 cups chopped onion   1 tsp. pepper
$\frac{1}{4}$ tsp. salt

Combine vegetables and salt. Let set overnight. Drain. Add all other ingredients and cook about 5 minutes. Put in hot jars and seal.

CANNED BEANS

$1\frac{1}{2}$ cups (scant) dry beans in quart jar
fill to neck with water
1 tsp. salt, opt.

Pressure can 90 minutes at 11 lbs. pressure or hot water bath 3 hours.

Hint: Most commercially canned beans contain sugar and various additives.

KETCHUP

Hint:
When harvesting small amounts of to-matoes, cut them up ready to cook. Put them in plastic bags and freeze. When ready to make ketch-up or pizza sauce, thaw overnight. Drain juice off and cook pulp.

1 - 2 hot peppers, without seeds   1 onion, sliced
1 clove garlic   4 quarts tomato chunks
1 tsp. pickling spice

Cook until soft. Pour clear juice off top. Put pulp through Victorio strainer.

In blender, mix:
$^1/_2$ cup white grape juice concentrate $^3/_4$ cup vinegar
1 tsp. cloves   1 tsp. cinnamon
1 tsp. dry mustard   1 Tbsp. salt
($^1/_2$ tsp. red pepper if hot peppers are not available.)
3 - 6 Tbsp. cornstarch or clear jel

In a large kettle bring juice to a boil. Stir blended ingredients in. Cook, stirring constantly, for 2 minutes, or longer if thicker ketchup is desired. Pour into hot jars and seal.

Note: After cooking 2 minutes, I like to put the ketchup in a roaster in the oven, uncovered. Bake 325 - 350° F. for 3 hours or until desired consistency. Stir occasionally. It will be a little thicker after it cools.

Note: Roma tomatoes are preferable for ketchup and pizza sauce. The end prod-uct is thicker.

PIZZA SAUCE

Heat in large kettle:
4 quarts tomato juice   1 onion, finely cut
1 tsp. oregano   1 tsp. black pepper
1 tsp. garlic salt   2 Tbsp. salt
$^1/_2$ tsp. Tobasco sauce or red pepper

Thicken with clear jel or cornstarch mixed in water. Bring to a boil. Cold pack for 30 minutes.

SALSA

8 quarts tomatoes   2 tsp. garlic powder
4 cups onions   2 tsp. paprika
4 cups green peppers   4 tsp. oregano
4 jalapeno peppers (remove seeds if you don't like it so hot)
1 tsp. chili powder   (or) 2 Tbsp. crushed red pepper
5 Tbsp. frozen white grape juice conc. 5 - 6 Tbsp. cornstarch
                         ¹/₄ cup vinegar

   Finely chop vegetables or chop in blender in small batches at a
time. Leave a little juice in bottom each time to start new batch.
Always put some tomatoes in first. Dump vegetables in a large kettle.
Bring to a boil and add spices and white grape juice. Dissolve cornstarch in vinegar. Stir into vegetables. Cook 5 minutes. Fill warm jars
and seal.

TOMATO JUICE COCKTAIL

Ripe tomatoes, quartered but not peeled - enough to almost fill an 8
         quart pot (about 8 lbs.)
2 medium onions, peeled and chopped
4 stalks celery with most of leaves on, cut in short pieces
2 small to medium carrots with tops on, chopped
1 hot pepper - adjust according to hotness desired
4 cloves garlic   1 bouquet parsley
1 Tbsp. salt   1 tsp. pepper
¹/₂ tsp. oregano, opt.

> **Note:** Never do just plain tomato juice. Tomato Juice Cocktail makes delicious soups and is also wonderful for drinking.

   Place tomatoes in 8 quart pot, mashing them as you go to form
juice. Add remaining ingredients *(see note below)*. Simmer over low
heat until vegetables are tender. Put through food mill or Victorio
strainer. Put hot into jars and process 15 minutes.

Note: (If using a food mill it works best to puree the raw vegetables
in the blender. Pour them over the tomatoes in the pot and simmer
until tomatoes are soft. With the Victorio strainer, the vegetables just
need to be chopped.)

   Vary the vegetables to your liking. The secret to this delicious juice
is that no water is added; it is all pure juice.

CHILI SOUP (TO CAN)

4 lbs. ground beef, browned
1 large onion, diced and sauted
14 cups beans
 2 tsp. oregano
34 cups (8¹/₂ quarts) Tomato Juice Cocktail *(see recipe on preceding page).*

4 Tbsp. chili powder
3 Tbsp. salt
3 tsp. thyme

Mix all ingredients. Pour into quart jars.
Pressure can 90 minutes at 11 lb. pressure; or cold pack 3 hours.

Yield: 14 quarts

CANNING MEAT

Pack ground beef, chunk beef, or chicken into pint or quart jars. Do not add water. Add ¹/₂ - 1 tsp. salt to each jar. Seal and process in pressure canner 90 minutes at 10 lbs. pressure (or) hot water bath for 3 hours.

FREEZING CARROTS (FOR CASSEROLES)

Carrots can be finely diced and blanched and then frozen in pints to add to casseroles and soups.

FREEZING PEPPERS (FOR PIZZA, ETC.)

Green peppers can be finely chopped and frozen.
Put 1 or 2 Tbsp. on pieces of saran and wrap individually.
Put the packets into a larger container.
Just take out a packet to use when making pizza, etc.

APPENDIX

Making the Transition

What to do if your family resists change:

- In the beginning try decreasing the sugar by ½, and add ½ substitute sweetener like fruit juice concentrate, barley malt or stevia. When you are used to that, slowly decrease to ¼ the amount.

- When converting a recipe that calls for honey, substitute ½ the amount of fruit juice concentrate. (Be sure to check the label - some juices have sugar!) Welsh is usually O.K.

- Keep using less sugar and more substitute.

- By the time you are using all substitute sweetener, you can start backing off on the quantity you are using.

- Choose recipes using nuts, dates, raisins, apples, or other fruits. They have a natural sweetening effect. Oatmeal in baked goods also seems to give a sweeter taste.
- For a sweeter finished product, in recipes calling for fruit juice, you can substitute frozen concentrate instead.

What if your family doesn't like the taste of alternate sweeteners?
Cut down gradually on the sugar, but do not use an alternate sweetener.

Got that low "bottomed out" feeling?
Try eating more frequently. Try protein snacks such as nuts and seeds.
Always be sure to eat before your "low" time comes, because the "lows" are exhausting the adrenals, as well as other organs of the body. If your low feeling comes 3 hours after eating, be sure to snack at 2½ hours after a meal. If it comes 4 hours after eating, snack at 3½ hours, and so on.

Be sure to go easy on fruit - even wholesome, fresh, homegrown fruit. Fruit contains **"simple sugars"**, and simple sugars do not need digestion, so it passes into the bloodstream too rapidly, and so the "HIGH - low" cycle starts all over again.

Be sure to eat a protein snack with your fruits - preferably nuts or seeds. Seeds such as pumpkin, sunflower, sesame, etc.

Cheese and animal protein also works, but has a tendency to overwork the kidneys and liver if too much is eaten.

Be sure you have lots of fiber in your diet! - very important with fruits. The more fiber you eat with your fruits, the slower the rate that the sugars enter the bloodstream. In other words, fiber controls the speed at which the body absorbs carbohydrates.

BEWARE! it is popular to juice fruits to make easy-to-drink juices. Juicing removes the fiber, which we hypoglycemics and diabetics need to control the rate at which we absorb the natural sugars in the fruit. Juice made with a regular juicer is a concentrated food that is very healing, but for the person with low blood sugar (hypoglycemia) or diabetes, it also allows the sugars to enter the bloodstream too rapidly.

The VITAMIX juicer is OK, because it leaves in all the fiber.

Foods that are high in fiber? Beans, lentils, split peas, nuts, seeds, whole grains, vegetables, and fruits are all high in fiber. Millet, bran, dried figs, sunflower seeds, and macadamia nuts have especially high amounts.

One Tbsp. of oat bran with meals will slow down sugar absorption dramatically.

Do not get discouraged! Changing to healthy eating takes time. The complete change may take years.

The day will come when sweets may tempt you, but when you eat them, they won't taste nearly as good as you thought they would. You will have learned to appreciate the taste of good wholesome food!

A Monster with Many Names

Following are some of the names for various kinds of sugar that you may find on food labels:

sucrose

glucose

lactose

dextrose

levulose

karo syrup

corn syrup

corn sweetener

maple sugar

cane sugar

cane syrup

raw sugar

sorbitol

polysorbate

Raw sugar is 97 - 99 percent sucrose.

The above sugars are basically <u>simple sugars,</u> which means they do not need to be digested, and for that reason they pass into the bloodstream very quickly. That is why they are so dangerous to someone with hypoglycemia or diabetes. They get too much sugar too fast.

SOME SWEETENERS AND WHAT THEY ARE MADE UP OF:

Molasses: A by-product of cane and beet sugar, and contains from 36 to 50 percent sugar.

Honey   Made up of the **simple sugars,** dextrose and levulose.

Blackstrap   A low grade molasses.

Fructose   Same as levulose, and is as much as $1^3/_4$ times as sweet as cane sugar. Fructose digests more slowly, therefore it is not absorbed into the bloodstream so rapidly.

WHOLE GRAINS, VERSUS REFINED GRAIN PRODUCTS

Whole grains   contain the entire grain kernel (bran, germ, and endosperm).
Refined grains (white flour, etc.) have the bran and germ removed to lengthen shelf life. Most of the nutrients are found in the bran and germ.

Whole grain flours, in comparison to refined white flours, slow down the rate at which sugars enter the bloodstream.

Store whole grain flour in the refrigerator or freezer.

Be a Label Reader

Many foods have sugar hidden in them!
The following <u>**almost always**</u> contain sugar:

bologna
ham
sausage
wieners
bacon
pepperoni

You can have your own variety meats processed. Just ask your butcher to leave out the sugar.

Following are examples of some foods that <u>**sometimes do and sometimes don't**</u> have sugar hiding in them:

crackers
salt
spaghetti sauce
pizza sauce
mayonnaise
juice concentrates
canned fruit juices
coconut
kidney beans
breaded fish
peanut butter
pre-basted turkey
pineapple

(Hint)   Some brands of pineapple are naturally sweeter tasting than others. **Liberty Gold** is quite sweet. **Dole** is also sweeter than many other brands.

Check the special diet section at your grocery store for sugar- free foods, but watch those labels carefully!

Following are some foods available in health food stores that may help in turning out tasty meals, but check labels - some may contain honey:

ketchup
mayonnaise
fakin' bacon bits
wieners
bologna
Vogue instant chicken or beef flavored base

Substitute Sweeteners
To be used with caution:

juice concentrates
barley malt
rice syrup
date sugar
dried fruit
molasses
malt syrup
maltose
malt

Watch out for barley malt with corn syrup; also carob chips, sweetened with corn and barley malt syrup. Limit to special occasions or serving to guests.

Rice syrup may be used in place of barley malt or stevia in any of our recipes.

Artificial Sweeteners

Use of **"Aspartame"** (Equal and NutraSweet), **"Splenda"** (sucralose), **Saccharin, Cyclamates, and Sweet'N'Lo** should be limited to special occasions.

Suggestion: Use 1/2 unsweetened flavored gelatin if it is available at your local bulk food or health food store. Experiment using fruit juices and unflavored gelatin.

During the time of transition, try using part NutriSweet jello and part fruit juice and gelatin, gradually using less jello and more gelatin and juice.

4 Mischievous Troublemakers

(For the hypoglycemic and diabetic)

1. **<u>Nicotine</u>** - This can include inhaled smoke from others.

2. **<u>Caffeine -</u>** This includes coffee, chocolate, cocoa, pop, and store tea like Lipton, etc.

    Garden tea and herbal teas are healthy.

    Carob chips, carob powder, etc. can be substituted for chocolate and cocoa. Carob chips with barley malt are good. But be careful! Some carob chips contain sugar. If melting carob chips, use barley malt sweetened carob chips. The unsweetened usually don't melt properly.

3. **<u>Sugar -</u>** Check information throughout this book.

4. **<u>Stress -</u>** It is impossible to live stress free in the fast paced society we live in, but it is possible to cut down on stress. Also there are supplements available that can help.

    Any of the above 4 can have much the same effect on you, so sometimes it is difficult to detect which of the culprits is making you ill.

--Milk Allergy--

When a recipe calls for milk and no substitute is given (such as pumpkin pie), you can substitute rice or soy milk. In many recipes fruit juice may also be substituted.

In many recipes, cheese can be substituted with tofu. You may need to wean your family gradually from cheese by using part cheese and part tofu in the beginning.

Many health food stores also carry soy cheeses.

Chronic earache?   Phlegm?   Colds?
or   A.D.D.?

The #1 suspect is **dairy products,** and #2 is **wheat products.** If your child is off these 2 foods for several weeks to a month, and the problem still exists, check the section **"MORE ON ALLERGIES".**

Colic in nursing babies can often be eliminated by the mother getting off dairy products. If the colic persists after the mother has been off dairy products for several weeks, then check the section **"MORE ON ALLERGIES".**

If the mother does not use dairy products during the next pregnancy, the baby is not nearly so likely to have milk allergies.

More on Allergies

Many persons with hypoglycemia have food allergies. It is now thought by some doctors that it is the allergies that cause the hypoglycemia, instead of the other way around; and they are having good success in treating the hypoglycemic by eliminating the allergy foods. Many of these allergies have hidden delayed reactions, which makes them very hard to detect. To make sure you are suspecting the right foods, we would recommend you have the Ig G ELISA allergy blood test done.

In looking for allergies, following is a list of the 7 most suspect foods:

> dairy
> eggs
> peanuts
> corn
> citrus
> soy
> wheat

For more information about delayed reaction food allergies and the Ig G ELISA blood test, call IMMUNO LABORATORIES AT 1-800-231-9197.

Egg Substitutes:

ENER-G makes an egg replacer containing potato starch that you may want to try.

What works best for us is: one ripe medium size mashed banana substituted for each egg.

Two Tbsp. applesauce substituted for each egg also works quite well in cookies.

Monosodium Glutamate

MSG (monosodium glutamate) is known to cause the same reactions in children as food allergies.

In adults and children it may cause migraine headaches, asthma, or depression.

It is a flavor enhancer found in spices, processed, packaged, and canned foods.

Many restaurants add MSG to their foods to enhance the taste.

MSG is not always listed in the ingredients of foods. Hydrolyzed vegetable protein may contain up to 20% MSG and not need to be listed. Hydrolyzed vegetable protein may also be listed simply as "natural flavorings".

It may be derived from soy, wheat, or seaweed.

For more information, including lists of restaurants and foods containing MSG, read: **"IN BAD TASTE - THE MSG SYNDROME"** by **George R. Schwartz, M.D.,** available at your public library.

–No Salt or Low Salt–

TIPS FOR "NO SALT" COOKING:

Using waterless cookware and cooking as nearly waterless as possible leaves the flavor in the food.

Cook until just tender crisp. Mushy food tastes flat.

Can your own meats and vegetables without salt. Most commercially canned foods are high in salt or sodium.

Make your own homemade noodles without salt. *(See recipe)*

Use broth from your canned meats to cook pastas, rice, etc.

Adding lots of celery, onion, peppers, or garlic to your food, also tomato juice cocktail *(See recipe),* makes it more tasty.

Barbecue meats plain or brush with salt free butter and, or vinegar.

Try pineapple juice on chicken; or lemon or pineapple juice on broiled fish.

For tastier foods try hot spices like cajun; or try Mrs. Dash.

CHECK LABELS: Some spices and "salt substitutes" have salt or sodium hiding in them.

SOME FOODS WITH VERY HIGH SALT CONTENT: bologna, ham, wieners, sausage, bacon, cheese, commercially canned soups.

TIPS FOR "LOW SALT" COOKING:

All the above tips apply to "low salt" cooking also.

Salt vegetables after they are cooked. They will need less. Mushy overcooked foods require more salt.

If using salted canned food items, rinse them off with water before preparing. (I put foods like tuna in a strainer and run water over it.)

Avoid instant hot cereals, and most cold cereals.

Omit or cut in half the amount of salt called for in a recipe.

Try Bio Salt (found in health food stores).

--~Resources--~

NATURE'S MARKET (no mail orders)
4860 E. Main Street, Berlin, Ohio 44610

Stevia herb, stevia extract, rice syrup, and barley malt;

Rice milk and soy milk;

Malt sweetened carob chips, unsweetened, or dairy free carob chips;

Vogue instant chicken, beef, or vegetable flavored base;

Sugar free wieners, bologna, and fakin' bacon; ketchup and mayonnaise, Ezekiel bread; corn flakes, crispy brown rice cereal, and many more cereals;

Beans, grains, and seeds in bulk;

Unsulphured dried fruits and nuts;

Sprouting seeds; carob powder; xanthan gum; Bio salt, and much more.

BERRY'S FISH AND HERB FARM   937-666-6107
P.O. Box 263
Middleburg, OH 43336

Stevia herb, Stevia extract, Stevia leaves, Liquid stevia

C. F. SAUER CO.   www.dukesmayo.com
                        800-688-5676 or 804-359-5786
2000 W. Broad Street
Richmond, Va. 23220

Duke's mayonnaise - sugar free; shipped in cases of 4 quarts each.

AMSTUTZ PANTRY   330-857-8159
15893 Baumgartner Rd.
Dalton, OH 44618

They ship. Call or write for a price list.

Brown rice, Barley, Dried beans, Lentils

Unsweetened carob chips, Carob powder

Raw nuts and seeds, Unsweetened pure peanut butter

Fruit juice sweetened jam, Sugar free apple butter

Pomona's Universal Pectin, Powdered barley malt

Stevia extract *(white)*, Stevia Herb *(green powder)*

"Real" salt, Whole grain flours, Whole grain pastas

ENER-G FOODS   800-331-5222
5960f First Avenue South
P. O. Box 84487
Seattle, WA 98124

They carry a selection of alternate grains, mixes, etc., also egg replacer.

KITCHEN SPECIALTIES AND GRANARY   419-542-6275
09264 Fountain Street Rd.
P.O. Box 100
Mark Center, Ohio 43536

Juicers, grain mills, sprouters, meat grinders, pasta machines, dehydrators, water distillers; also beans, grains, pasta, flour and more.

POMONA'S UNIVERSAL PECTIN   413-772-6816
www.permaculture.net/Pomona/

www.urbanhomemaker.com/items/canning/pomonasuniversalpectin.htm

WAL-MART SUPER CENTERS

Duke's mayonnaise, sugar free bacon, cold pressed extra virgin olive oil, "Star Kist" Gourmet Choice Tuna, Juicy Juice Fruit Punch, Rice Milk, Unsweetened Frozen Fruit Juice Concentrates.

FOOD LION GROCERY STORES

Duke mayonnaise

SMITH'S BULK FOOD 330-857-1132

5413 S. Mount Eaton Rd.
Dalton, Ohio 44618

They ship. Call or write for price list.

Brown rice, Barley, Dried beans, Lentils

Malt sweetened carob chips, Unsweetened carob chips, Carob powder, Lecithin granules,

Raw nuts and seeds, Unsweetened pure peanut butter

Fruit juice sweetened jam, Sugar free apple butter

Stevia Extract *(white)*, Barley Malt powder

Whole grain flours, Whole grain pastas

SMUCKERS

Unsweetened peanut butter, Simply 100% fruit jam, R.W. Knudsen pure unsweetened fruit juices.

Available in their retail store at Orrville, Ohio; in your local grocery; or call 1-800-742-6729 to order.

Reference Books

Check for availability at your local library.

THE ALLERGY SELF-HELP BOOK by Sharon Faelten and the Editors of Prevention Magazine

DR. BRALY'S FOOD ALLERGY AND NUTRITION REVOLUTION by James Braly, MD.

THE YEAST CONNECTION HANDBOOK by Daniel Crook

WHAT THE BIBLE SAYS ABOUT HEALTHY LIVING by Rex Russel, MD.

IN BAD TASTE - THE MSG SYNDROME by George R. Schwartz, MD.

LOW BLOOD SUGAR HANDBOOK by Ed and Patricia Krimmel

THE DO'S AND DON'TS OF LOW BLOOD SUGAR- AN EVERYDAY GUIDE FOR HYPOGLYCEMIA by Roberta Ruggiero

HYPOGLYCEMIA AND DIABETES-A WELLNESS GUIDE by Freda Whalen, R.M.T., with Gilbert Manso, M.D.

Index

BREAKFASTS AND BEVERAGES

BREADS

MAIN DISHES

MEATS

SOUPS AND SANDWICHES

VEGETABLES

SALADS AND SALAD DRESSINGS

CAKES AND CUPCAKES

COOKIES, BROWNIES AND BARS

DESSERTS

ICE CREAM AND FROZEN DESSERTS

PIES

MISCELLANEOUS

SNACKS

CANNING AND FREEZING

APPLE VIEW PUBLICATIONS
4495 CUTTER ROAD
APPLE CREEK OH 44606

Date:_____

Ship to: Name_____
(Please print)

Street_____

City_____State_____Zip_____

Please send me:

____copies of <u>WOW! This Is Sugar Free Cookbook</u> $10.95 each _____

____copies of <u>WOW! Low Cholesterol & Sugar Free Cookbook</u> $10.95 each _____
(Stevia sweetener & tips on lowering cholesterol the natural way)

____copies of <u>WOW! This Is Allergy Free Cookbook</u> $10.95 each _____
(Stevia sweetener & 4-day rotation diet)

Shipping and handling for first book $2.50 _____

Canadian Orders add additional $4.50 (U.S. Funds only) $4.50 _____

Shipping for each additional book to same address $.75 _____

Orders will be shipped parcel post, book rate
(or)   Add extra for UPS (U.S. only) $1.00 _____

TOTAL _____

Make checks payable to:
APPLE VIEW PUBLICATIONS

Dealers and distributors, write for more information.